MONEY MATTERS:
RETIREMENT AND BEYOND

AUSTRALIA
LBC Information services
Sydney

CANADA AND THE USA
Carswell
Toronto

NEW ZEALAND
Brooker's
Auckland

SINGAPORE AND MALASIA
Thomson Information (S.E. Asia)
Singapore

MONEY MATTERS: RETIREMENT AND BEYOND

by

Valerie J. Smart C.A., ATII, TEP
PricewaterhouseCoopers

EDINBURGH
W. GREEN/Sweet & Maxwell
1998

First published, 1998

Published in 1998 by W. Green & Son Limited of
21 Alva Street,
Edinburgh EH2 4PS

Typeset by Hewer Text Limited, Edinburgh
109 Ferry Road, Edinburgh EH6 4ET

Printed and bound in Great Britain by
Redwood Books, Trowbridge, Wiltshire

No natural forests were destroyed to make this product;
only farmed timber was used and replanted

A CIP catalogue record of this book is available
from the British Library

ISBN 0 414 01170 8

© The Institute of Chartered Accountants in Scotland 1998

The moral rights of the author have been asserted

All rights reserved. United Kingdom statutory material
in this publication is acknowledged as Crown copyright.

No part of this publication may be reproduced or transmitted in any form or by any means, or stored in any retrieval system of any nature without prior written permission, except for permitted fair dealing under the Copyright, Designs and Patents Act 1988, or in accordance with the terms of a licence issued by the Copyright Licensing Agency in respect of photocopying and/or reprographic reproduction. Applications for permission for other use of copyright material including permission to reproduce extracts in other published work shall be made to the publisher. Full acknowledgment of author, publisher and source must be given.

PREFACE

This book is intended for practitioners in both the legal and accountancy professions, students in these professions and those who are elderly themselves or help elderly relatives and wish to be more informed about the issues they should address. Like any general work of this size, it does not pretend to cover all the issues in depth but is intended to alert its readers to those areas where more specialist professional advice is required.

Thanks are due to all those who read and commented on the contents of the book, including my sister Margaret Smart and staff at PricewaterhouseCoopers—Andy McKinnell, Blair Miller and Jamie Younger. Thanks are also due to Anne Bryce who commissioned its production on behalf of the Institute of Chartered Accountants of Scotland. The views expressed in the book are, however, the author's alone.

The law is stated as at July 31, 1998.

Valerie J. Smart c.a., atii, tep

CONTENTS

Preface v
Introduction 1
1. Retiral and income tax 3
2. Pensions 19
3. Income in retirement 49
4. Disposing of a business 79
5. Estate planning 93
6. State provision for old age 117
7. Death 129
Appendix 141
Index 153

INTRODUCTION

Improvements in healthcare have dramatically increased our lifespans over the last century. Many of us can now look forward to almost as long a period in retirement as we spend in work.

Retirement marks a major change in our lives. Finances change, often dramatically. Many financial events, such as paying off a mortgage, are geared towards retirement. Yet many people fail to plan adequately for this period of their lives and the financial changes it brings.

We need to consider the issues of this stage in our life cycle—how will we spend our leisure time; how will we fund our new lifestyle in retirement; can we afford to pay for care if needed in old age; who will inherit our estate; and how much of that estate will the Government claim?

This book examines how to plan for the financial aspects of later years—before giving up work, during retirement itself and on death.

Chapter 1

RETIRAL AND INCOME TAX

No one is sure how many people in Britain pay the wrong amount of tax each year. What is clear is that many people in retirement who have their tax affairs checked will find they are paying an incorrect amount of tax. The reasons are not hard to find. **1.1**

People who are in employment have tax deducted from their earnings by their employer under the PAYE system. Each year they will have had a Notice of Coding and provided this is correct, the appropriate amount of income tax will have been collected on each pay day. When individuals retire, they may find that they have multiple sources of income. They are much more likely to have investment income. All of this complicates the way in which PAYE operates, increasing the chances that too much or too little tax is paid. **1.2**

The tax system changes continually, making it hard for the average taxpayer to know what his responsibilities are and what opportunities are available. Human resource departments may go out of their way to help employees but often have little contact with pensioners. The self-employed may have decided to dispense with the help of an accountant when they no longer carry on a business. Just when advice is less readily available, the retired may well find they face a more complex tax situation than they ever imagined. If worries about tax liabilities are to be avoided, it is worth spending time at the outset of retirement to understand what is required and how to deal with it. This chapter looks at income tax issues facing the elderly. **1.3**

Receipt of a pension

1.4 Most individuals who have reached state pension age will receive a pension from the United Kingdom Government. No tax is deducted from this pension at source.

1.5 Depending on their circumstances, individuals may receive a variety of other pensions provided for them based on former employment or occupation. Thus any one individual may have several pensions in payment at any one point in time. Pensions are provided in a variety of ways, and this is explored in more depth at a later point in this book. Commonly a pension annuity is purchased which provides regular monthly income. If the source of the pension is an occupational pension scheme, then PAYE should be operated at the point of payment so that tax is deducted at source. If the pension is purchased out of the proceeds of a personal pension plan, tax is also deducted under PAYE by the company from which the pension annuity is purchased. This applies to personal pensions paid after 6 April 1995, where previously only tax at the basic rate was deducted from such annuities at source. Pension annuities purchased from retirement annuity contracts continue to have tax deducted at the basic rate only. Other types of pension fall mainly under the PAYE system, *e.g.* unapproved pension arrangements or voluntary pensions, but pensions from overseas sources may have no tax deducted at all or may have foreign tax deducted.

1.6 To summarise, each separate pension may be taxed at source as set out in Table 1.1.

1.7 PAYE operates best where there is only one source of earnings. To operate properly where there are multiple sources, it is essential that allowances, other tax deductions and reliefs and tax rates are allocated appropriately and a separate Notice of Coding needs to be issued for each source. Even then, estimates may need to be used in arriving at the tax rates or allowances due, and since this is done before the start of the tax year any inaccuracy will result in the wrong tax being deducted.

TABLE 1.1

Not taxed at source	Taxed under PAYE system	Basic rate tax deducted	Foreign tax deducted
State retirement pension	Occupational pensions	Retirement annuity pension	Foreign source pensions
Foreign source pensions	Personal pensions		
	Unapproved pensions		
	Voluntary pensions		

For pensions not taxed under PAYE, too much or too little tax may be deducted at source. To have any chance of the tax system deducting the correct amount of tax at source, it is vital the tax office is informed immediately of all sources of pensions and of any change in circumstances. Even then, it is frequently the case that tax deducted at source from pensions must be amended to the correct amount at the end of the tax year by filing a tax return.   **1.8**

Other income

Those in retirement are also likely to have sources of unearned income. This may come from investment of a lump sum paid on retirement from a pension scheme, from savings or from some other source. While most sources of investment income have tax deducted at source this is not true of all. Furthermore, the taxpayer may be due to pay less tax than is deducted or, if a higher rate taxpayer, more.   **1.9**

Self-assessment

One common problem is that individuals often expect the Inland Revenue to take the initiative when it comes to collecting the correct amount of tax. Far from being the case, the onus is on the individual to notify the Inland Revenue that tax is due to be paid or reclaimed. Failure to notify the   **1.10**

Inland Revenue that tax is due by the due date can be expensive, as interest and penalties can then be added to any tax bill.

1.11 An individual is required to notify the Inland Revenue that he is chargeable to tax unless his full liability has been satisfied by deduction at source. This means that those with untaxed income, chargeable gains or individuals who are liable to higher rate tax fall among the group who should notify liability to tax if a tax return has not been issued to them automatically each tax year. The deadline for advising the Inland Revenue that tax is due is October 5 following the end of the tax year. If a taxpayer who is not sent a tax return fails to give notice and fails to pay any tax due by the following January 31, he is liable to a penalty of up to the amount of the unpaid tax. While this can be mitigated by the Inland Revenue, it remains potentially very expensive to fail to give notice of chargeability. If the October 5 deadline is missed it is therefore essential to calculate and pay all tax due by January 31.

1.12 If a tax repayment is due, it can be claimed by submitting a tax repayment claim form to an Inland Revenue repayment district. Alternatively if a tax return has been issued or if you ask for one, you can choose to self-assess your tax liability for the year and obtain repayment in this way.

1.13 Many retired taxpayers automatically receive a tax return each year, and those who notify chargeability should also receive a return to complete. The tax return must be fully completed and filed by the filing date which is normally January 31 following the end of the tax year. Where the tax return is issued after October 31, the deadline is three months from the date of issue.

1.14 There are two reasons why taxpayers may wish to file their return before this deadline. The first is that if the return is filed by September 30 (or two months after date of issue if later) the taxpayer is relieved from his obligation to self-assess his own tax bill and the Inland Revenue will do this for him. The second is that if he pays tax under PAYE and the underpayment for the year is less than £1,000 it is usually possible to have this collected through the PAYE system by adjusting the Notice of Coding from the start of the next tax year. This saves paying any underpayment in one lump sum. (If possible the Revenue extend this deadline to November 30 but will not guarantee the position and will not collect unpaid tax through PAYE on returns lodged after November.)

1.15 Those who file returns after September 30 must work out their own tax bill but in both cases any tax due must be paid by January 31 following the end of the tax year. If the tax is not paid on time interest is charged on the amount paid late. If the tax is paid after February 28 a surcharge of 5 per cent of the unpaid tax is added. This surcharge also bears interest. If tax is paid after July 31 the surcharge rises to 10 per cent of the unpaid tax.

1.16 The process of working out the tax bill and entering the figures on the tax return is known as self-assessment. In addition to working out the tax bill for the tax year to which the return relates, the process also determines the amount of tax which must be paid on account of the current tax year in which the return is filed.

1.17 Two payments on account of tax due must be made in respect of each tax year ending on April 5. The first payment is made on January 31 in the tax year (at the same time as any balance is paid in respect of the previous year), and the second payment is made on July 31 immediately following the end of the tax year. Working out the amount of each payment is straightforward in the first instance as it is linked to the tax bill for the prior year, and the amounts of the payments on account are included in the tax return to be filed for that earlier year. If the taxpayer has not previously had to self-assess payment of tax he will have no payments on account to make. If he has, he calculates his total tax bill less tax deducted from income at source for the last tax year. If this is less than £500, and is less than 20 per cent of the total tax bill he has no need to make any payments on account. If the excess is greater than either of these two limits, each payment on account required is 50 per cent of the excess.

1.18 *Example*:
Total tax due for 1997/98: £20,000
Tax deducted at source (including PAYE): £17,000
Excess: £3,000—tax payable January 31, 1999 (*less* payments on account for 1997/98)
This exceeds £500 *de minimis* limit
1998/99 first payment on account due January 31, 1999 = £1,500
1998/99 second payment on account due July 31, 1999 = £1,500

1.19 Of course, these payments on account may exceed the total tax liability expected for the tax year. This can happen when there is a change of circumstances. One of the most common changes of circumstances that might result in a reduction of tax payable is when income falls following retirement, so that a higher rate taxpayer becomes a basic rate taxpayer. Other examples are when income not taxed at source is switched into a source which is so taxed, or when the taxpayer is eligible for larger tax deductions than he received in the previous year. If the taxpayer believes that he will not be due to pay income tax for the year, or that his liability will be less than the payments on account otherwise due, he can apply to reduce the interim payments down to the level of tax he expects to be due for the whole year. Each payment on account is then set at 50 per cent of this sum.

1.20 There are procedures that must be followed and risks attaching to this process. It requires a formal tax claim to be made. Usually this can be included on the tax return for the prior year or alternatively a claim form SA 303 obtainable from the Inland Revenue can be submitted or the taxpayer can simply write to the Revenue setting out the grounds for his belief that the payments should be reduced. The reduction cannot be challenged by the Inland Revenue but if the reduction is too large and tax becomes payable when the taxpayer works out his self-assessment for the year, interest will be payable on the amount underpaid from the date on which the tax would have been due if the reduction had not been made. To stop abuse of the system, if the taxpayer makes a statement which is incorrect and does so deliberately (so it is fraudulent) or accidentally but as a result of negligence, he can be liable to a penalty of up to the amount of the difference between the payment on account that would have been due and the sum actually paid.

These rules mean that in the year of retirement, great care needs to be taken to forecast as accurately as possible the level of tax that will be payable, so that payments on account can be adjusted appropriately and any tax overpaid is refunded at the earliest possible date. **1.21**

Tax deductions

It is important when filling in the tax return that all available tax deductions are claimed. For the elderly, one of the main areas of difficulty is working out the level of tax allowances that are due and claiming them. **1.22**

The normal allowance which is available to most United Kingdom taxpayers is the personal allowance. Set at £4,195 for 1998/99, the figure is usually announced in each Budget for the forthcoming year. If not changed by the Chancellor, like all other allowances it is increased automatically by inflation for each tax year. The allowance is available to both husband and wife to set against their own income but if either has insufficient income to cover the allowance the excess cannot be transferred to the other spouse. The allowance is given as a straight deduction from taxable income, so it reduces the tax liability at whatever marginal rate of tax would otherwise be suffered. **1.23**

Married couples (who are living together and not separated) also qualify for the married couple's allowance. Tax relief for this allowance is given in the form of a tax deduction. The value of the deduction is a reduction in the tax bill of £285 in 1998/99, but limited so that at most it reduces the tax bill to nil and cannot create a tax repayment. The deduction is based on an allowance of £1,900 for 1998/99. For 1998/99 the tax deduction is 15 per cent of this allowance, but this falls to 10 per cent from 1999/00. Unlike the personal allowance, the allowance itself is not deducted from taxable income. **1.24**

The allowance is given in the first instance to the husband, but the wife has the right to claim 50 per cent of the relief without her husband's agreement. If both spouses agree, they can jointly elect that the whole of the allowance will be **1.25** given to the wife (in which case the husband has the right to change his mind and claim up to one-half of the allowance back without his wife's agreement). A claim to transfer 50 per cent or all of the allowance in this way is beneficial if the husband pays insufficient tax to absorb the whole of the tax deduction. It is also made if the husband and wife want to keep their financial position strictly separated and for each to pay their separate share of the couple's tax bill. To make the claim, a Form 18 must be completed and lodged with the Inland Revenue before the start of the tax year from which it is to take effect. Thereafter it takes effect from year to year without a further claim until changed. As the claim must be made before the start of the year, accurate forecasting of income is needed to determine if a transfer is beneficial. The only exception is in the year of marriage when the claim can be made for the year in which the marriage takes place.

1.26 Although estimating income to determine if the allowance should be transferred in advance may be difficult, all is not lost if it turns out that the husband is unable to use the whole of the allowance. Provided the husband agrees, any balance of the reduction which he does not use can be transferred to his wife if she makes a claim to that effect. The claim must be made not later than five years after the normal tax payment date, *e.g.* for 1998/99 the claim must be made by January 31, 2005.

Age allowance

1.27 The personal allowance and married couple's allowance above are increased if two qualifying criteria—age and income level—are met. These increased allowances are known as age allowances. For the elderly, ensuring that the correct amount is claimed, and planning income to maximise the reliefs, can be extremely worthwhile in reducing the tax bill.

1.28 The allowances increase for two age bands—those aged 65 upwards and those aged 75 upwards. In the case of the personal allowance, the higher age allowance is available if the claimant was over 65 at any time within the tax year. In the case of the married couple's allowance, the higher allowance is available if *either* spouse was aged 65 or over at any time within the tax year. It is perfectly possible for a 63-year-old man to be entitled to claim the normal personal allowance but the higher married couple's allowance because his wife is aged 65 for example.

1.29 For 1998/99 the personal allowance is increased to £5,410 for those aged 65 or over and £5,600 for those aged 75 or over. In the case of the married couple's allowance the allowance is £3,305 for those where one spouse is aged 65 or more and £3,345 where either spouse is aged 75 or more.

1.30 When it comes to transferring the married couple's allowance to the wife, the transfer of 50 per cent or 100 per cent is limited to the basic allowance and not to the increased age element. However, if the transfer is claimed of the amount of the allowance unused by the husband, it is the full married couple's age allowance that can be transferred. These complex rules mean that some couples will need to review the position for each tax year both before it begins and again when it finishes.

1.31 The second criteria for claiming the higher age allowances is the income limit. The income level to be considered here is that of the claimant for the personal allowance but the husband for the married couple's allowance. Like the allowances themselves the income limit is set each year and increases in line with inflation if not adjusted by the Chancellor in his annual Budget. For 1998/99 the income limit was set at £16,200. Where the total taxable income exceeds that level, the excess is calculated and the increased allowances are reduced by 50 per cent of the excess until the basic level of allowances are reached. This excess is used to reduce the personal allowance first, and only if there is still an excess is the married couple's allowance then reduced. The undernoted example shows how this process works:

Husband aged 76, total income £19,500
Wife aged 72, total income £16,500

	£	£
Husband's personal allowance		5,600
Income	19,500	
less limit	16,200	
Excess	3,300	
Allowance reduction 50% (limited to £1,405)		1,405
Age allowance due (not less than basic allowance)		4,195
Married couple's allowance		3,345
Income	19,500	
less limit	16,200	
Excess	3,300	
50%	1,650	
Reduction in personal allowance, above	1,405	
Allowance reduction		245
Age married couple's allowance due		3,100
Wife's personal allowance		5,410
Income	16,500	
less limit	16,200	
Excess	300	
Allowance reduction 50%		150
Age allowance due		5,260

1.32 It will be readily appreciated that there is a lot of scope for error in working out allowances and due care is required. Moreover, where tax is collected from pensions and earnings under the PAYE system, the code number used to collect tax has to include the allowances due. Where the allowances are subject to an adjustment for the income level, it follows that the Notice of Coding will have to be estimated since total income will only be known at the end of the tax year. In most cases that means that the tax deducted will have to be adjusted by self-assessment at the end of the tax year. Lack of awareness of these issues is one of the biggest causes of incorrect tax being paid and many taxpayers inadvertently overpay each year. With the penalties for failure to notify chargeability to tax described above being in operation it is just as financially expensive to underpay by mistake. For that reason most pensioners would be well advised to check their tax liability in full each year.

Planning income levels

Apart from the complexity of the tax system in relation to these allowances, there is considerable scope for planning income to maximise the reliefs due. Pension income is usually fixed, although sometimes there is scope to determine when the pension is first drawn. However, careful investment of lump sums can enable an investment income to be achieved in a form which does not count as taxable income for allowances purposes. Income which is tax-free is rare and tax sheltered investments may be particularly valuable to the elderly for this reason. Examples of investments in this category are personal equity plans and tax-exempt special savings accounts until April 5, 1999, their replacement the independent savings account, and national savings certificates.

1.33

In the case of a purchased life annuity a proportion of each payment is treated as capital not subject to income tax and hence that capital element does not count as income for allowances purposes. Single-premium life assurance bonds (often called investment bonds) are another example of an investment that can be used to maximise allowances. Here the tax liability on encashment of the bond is deferred until the whole bond matures or is encashed, but up to 5 per cent of the original investment can be withdrawn annually for up to 20 years to provide an income without counting towards total income for tax purposes. At a more sophisticated level shares in split capital investment trusts can be used to control income levels. Anyone providing investment advice to those over age 65 needs to consider not just the ordinary merit of each type of investment but also how it will impact on their tax situation.

1.34

In the case of married couples, thought should be given to transferring investment income between spouses in such a way as to ensure one or both qualify for the higher age allowances. Such income transfers can also allow married couples to double up on the use of lower and basic rate tax bands and avoid being subject to tax at higher rates. To be effective, such transfers must constitute an outright gift. This

1.35

means that the right to income alone cannot be gifted so, for example, a husband cannot undertake to pay his wife an annuity. The gift must be of capital which carries a right to the whole of the income. It must not be subject to conditions nor must the property or anything derived from it be payable to the donor spouse under any circumstances. These rules mean that thought must be given to the wider issues before such gifts are advised. Is there adequate protection from the recipient becoming incapacitated? Is there any danger of the marriage breaking up? If so, would this affect the financial division on separation? Does the transfer affect rights of succession by the family on death? Does it affect the division of the combined estate for inheritance tax purposes and the consequential liability to tax on death? Does it give rise to other taxes? While capital gains tax is not charged on transfers between spouses, and the gifts are exempt from inheritance tax unless one spouse is United Kingdom domiciled and the other is not, there can be consequential results which must be thought about. It is important not to let the income tax benefits drive matters without appropriate attention to the other consequences, but nonetheless substantial tax savings can be achieved if appropriate planning is entered into.

Jointly held investments

1.36 As a result of the difficulties and potential dangers of transferring capital outright between spouses, another option which can be more attractive is to put investments into joint names. Where property is held in joint names, husband and wife are each treated as entitled to an equal share of any income from it. For example, if a building society account was held in joint names, and interest of £500 was paid on the account, each would be treated as though they had received interest of £250.

1.37 It may be that in reality each owns the property in different shares. For example, suppose that a couple own a flat which they rent out. The wife has 25 per cent ownership and the husband 75 per cent. If they do nothing, rental income will be deemed to arise to each of them on a 50:50 basis.

Alternatively they could make a declaration to the Inland Revenue of their actual beneficial ownership. In the illustration above, the wife would be taxed on 25 per cent of the rent and the husband on 75 per cent. Note that a declaration must correspond to actual beneficial ownership and intermediate figures are not permitted. The declaration must be made on a Form 17 and notice given to the Inland Revenue within 60 days of the date of the declaration. The notice only has effect on income arising after the date of the declaration. This means it is important when acquiring new sources of income in joint but unequal shares that prompt action is taken if income is not to be taxed on a 50:50 basis. Effectively declarations cannot be backdated.

1.38 These rules do mean that it is worthwhile for married couples in retirement to look carefully at how they hold their investments and whether restructuring the holdings means that they will obtain better tax allowances and pay less tax.

Other allowances

1.39 Other allowances that are particularly relevant to the elderly are blind person's allowance and widow's bereavement allowance. Blind person's allowance is available to a person registered as blind and is given as a deduction from total taxable income. The allowance has been set at £1,330 for 1998/99. If the claimant is a married man whose wife lives with him, but he is unable to use the whole of the allowance because of an insufficiency of income, the balance can be transferred to his wife. Similarly a wife can transfer any balance of her unused allowance to her husband.

1.40 Widow's bereavement allowance is available to a widow in the tax year in which her husband dies and in the following year unless she remarries. The allowance is equivalent to the basic married couple's allowance and is given in the form of a tax reduction at the same rate as the married couple's allowance.

Medical insurance

1.41 During working life private medical insurance is often available as a benefit of employment, often at corporate rates. On retiral many people wish to continue this cover but have to shoulder the premiums themselves. For those aged 60 and above (or in the case of a married couple where the insurance covers both and one is aged 60 or over), tax relief was available on certain qualifying policies. This relief was abolished for new contracts taken out after July 2, 1997 and expires by April 6, 1999 for contracts taken out earlier. For those who still qualify, relief in 1998/99 is restricted to the basic rate of tax on gross premiums paid and is deducted at source when paying the premium.

Tax rates

1.42 Different tax rates apply to different levels and types of income. The tax rates for 1998/99 are:

Lower rate on first £4,300	20%
Basic rate on £4,301–£27,100	23%
Higher rate on excess over £27,100	40%

Income from dividends and interest on savings is taxed at 20 per cent instead of 23 per cent.

Receiving investment income gross

1.43 Some elderly retired people find themselves with very low incomes. Taking account of the high allowances they are entitled to, described above, they can find they are not due to pay any income tax at all. Any savings that are invested in a bank or a building society may earn interest. The normal rule is that tax must be deducted at source from such interest. However, individuals who do not pay tax can give notice to the bank or building society so that such income is paid gross. A registration form can usually be obtained from the bank or building society or Form R85 can be obtained from the Inland Revenue and completed. This is then handed in to the bank or building society who will thereafter pay interest gross. The benefit of having the income paid gross is improved cash flow and less administration in that there is no need to reclaim the tax deducted at source. If the individual subsequently finds that he is liable to tax because his income level has grown he must tell the bank or building society immediately so that he starts receiving interest net again. He must also pay any tax due on income not taxed erroneously by notifying chargeability and filing a self-assessment.

Some people are confused by the definition of a non-taxpayer. Pensioners often forget about their state pension which absorbs their personal allowance. Many think that if they do not pay more tax than is deducted from income at source they can apply to have interest paid gross. Others think that because their tax liability is less than the tax deducted at source and they are entitled to a tax repayment they can also apply. Both are wrong and the requirement is that the individual has no tax liability at all. Usually this arises because income is less than the personal allowances. In all other circumstances the interest must be paid under deduction of tax. **1.44**

Until April 6, 1998, interest from government securities (gilts) was also usually paid after deducting tax at the lower rate from the interest. There were some exceptions to this but from April 6, 1998, recipients, regardless of their tax status, receive the interest paid gross unless they ask for tax to be deducted at source. It is important to remember to include such gross income in the tax return at the end of the tax year. **1.45**

Living abroad

Some people decide that on retirement they wish to live abroad. Many factors should be appraised before the decision to move overseas is undertaken; among these is the tax consequences of such a move. **1.46**

If the move abroad is permanent, it may be that the individual ceases to be resident or ordinarily resident in the United Kingdom. While personal allowances are not generally available to non-residents to offset against United Kingdom **1.47** source income, this will not normally apply to people retiring abroad. Commonwealth citizens and nationals within the European Economic Area, residents of the Channel Islands and Isle of Man, and former Crown employees and their widows are all entitled to personal allowances as are former United Kingdom residents and their families who move abroad for the sake of their health.

1.48 Residence for tax purposes has a special meaning. An individual who is resident or ordinarily resident in the United Kingdom will be liable to tax on his worldwide income, whereas a non-resident will only be liable to tax on United Kingdom source income. If regular visits are made to the United Kingdom or only part of the year is spent abroad and part in the United Kingdom, it may be that the individual becomes resident in two countries. In that case there is the possibility of income being liable to tax in both jurisdictions, with relief being given under the terms of any tax treaty which exists or unilaterally by the United Kingdom.

1.49 An individual will always be United Kingdom resident if he is physically present in the United Kingdom for 183 days in any tax year. A day is measured according to whether the individual is present in the United Kingdom at the end of it. Even if the 183-day test is satisfied, an individual will still be resident in the United Kingdom if time spent in the United Kingdom exceeds an average of 91 days measured over not more than four tax years. Retaining property in the United Kingdom may be a factor in determining residence, depending on why it has been retained and whether it is available for use on any visits back to the United Kingdom. Determining residence is a difficult matter and specialist advice should usually be sought.

CHAPTER 2

PENSIONS

The British social security system provides a basic retirement **2.1**
pension for most people who spend their working life in the
United Kingdom. A great worry for many people is whether
this basic pension will provide an adequate and comfortable
level of income in old age. Few believe this will be the case,
and more and more people recognise the need to top up state
provision with some form of private provision. At Government level, consideration is being given to whether this top-up should be compulsory but no decision has yet been reached. Even if measures are taken to compel people to provide for their own pension in old age it will be many years before this makes a significant impact on pension levels. For those approaching retirement or who plan to retire early, it is vital to review pension provision and take advantage of any opportunities available to maximise pension provision if they hope to live in comfort in old age. This chapter looks at options available for pension provision.

Preparing for retirement

The range of private pension options available is consider- **2.2**
able and this range contributes to the complexity of the
United Kingdom pension scene. Each type of arrangement
has its own tax rules, which govern how the pension scheme
operates. If an individual has had one occupation all his
working career, he may only have one type of pension to
worry about. Nowadays most people will have changed jobs
at least once in their working life and may have migrated
from employed status to self-employed or vice versa. This
makes it likely that they will have more than one type of

scheme, and the way in which these interact will affect the total pension that can be provided at retirement.

2.3 Why is it so beneficial to provide for retirement through a pension scheme? The first reason is that contributions to pension schemes within the permitted limits qualify for tax relief. Contributions paid by employers on behalf of their employees are deductible from taxable profits, while the employee is not taxed on the benefit of the contribution. Contributions paid by individuals can be deducted from taxable income.

2.4 Secondly, income (other than dividends) and capital gains realised within the pension fund are not subject to tax so the value of the fund should accumulate quicker than if savings are made outside a pension scheme. (The tax credit attaching to dividends ceased to be recoverable by pension funds after July 1, 1997, effectively subjecting this part of the pension fund's income to tax.) When benefits are drawn in the form of a pension these are taxed at that time but sometimes at lower rates of tax than suffered when in full-time employment. In addition, most pension arrangements allow for pension to be commuted in exchange for a lump sum which is tax free within statutory limits.

2.5 The disadvantage is that investment in a pension scheme is very illiquid since in the case of approved schemes which qualify for these tax reliefs, the funds cannot be accessed until retirement age is reached. On the other hand, this can be regarded as a good thing as it stops the funds set aside for pension provision being used in any other way.

2.6 In an ideal world saving to provide for pension should start at an early age. In fact many people pay scant attention to pension provision until late in their working life. In the run up to retirement a review should be undertaken of the level of pension expected and a decision made on whether this provision can be topped up. To complete this exercise it is necessary to understand what types of pension provision are available, what the options are in relation to each, and how they interact.

Occupational pension schemes

The key requirement of an occupational pension scheme is that an employer must contribute to it on behalf of the employees. This means that it is not open to those who are self-employed, although it is the most common type of arrangement for employees. Employers are entitled to tax relief for the contributions they make to these schemes provided they meet certain conditions. These conditions govern the amount of pension that can be drawn at retirement age. The main conditions relevant to the individual pensioner are as follows:

2.7

- the sole purpose of the scheme must be to provide pension and similar benefits for the employee, widow or widower, children, dependants, and personal representatives. No one else can be provided for;
- any pension should be payable not earlier than age 50 (or earlier incapacity) and not later than age 75;
- the pension payable should not exceed one-sixtieth of the employee's final remuneration for each year of service up to a maximum of 40. This means that the maximum pension that can be provided is two-thirds of final salary;
- the widow's or widower's pension must not exceed two-thirds of the pension payable to the employee;
- the pension should not be commutable for a lump sum of more than three-eighths of final remuneration for each year of service up to a maximum of 40. The maximum lump sum that can be drawn in lieu of pension is therefore 1.5 times final salary;
- where an employee has two or more employments which are associated with one another, the position has to be looked at in aggregate;
- while the overall maximum of a pension of two-thirds final salary or a lump sum of 1.5 times final salary cannot be exceeded, schemes can allow these limits to be reached for service of less than 40 years;
- death in service benefits for a widow, child or dependant of the employee can also be provided as well as a death in service benefit of up to four times the employee's final remuneration exclusive of any refund of contributions.

2.8 In general, individuals who join occupational pension schemes after July 27, 1989 have a further limitation on the pension benefits that can be drawn. Those affected have final remuneration limited by an "earnings cap". Earnings above the level of the cap are disregarded in fixing the maximum benefits that can be taken. Unless the Chancellor of the Exchequer decides otherwise the level of the cap grows by inflation each tax year. For 1998/99 the maximum remuneration level is set at £87,600. Despite this disadvantage, there are more favourable early retirement limits under the rules that apply to pension schemes in the post-1989 regime. It is often possible for members who joined before July 27, 1989 to arrange for the post-1989 rules to be applied to take advantage of this, but the earnings cap will then apply.

2.9 These rules allow for a great deal of flexibility and not every pension scheme will allow the maximum benefits to be taken. A pension scheme that provides for the benefits to be expressed in pension terms is known as a defined benefits scheme—the employer will have to meet the cost of providing the benefits promised, whatever that might be. Other schemes work on the basis of defined contributions—the employer only promises to make contributions up to a certain level and the employee can then draw benefits up to the maximum limits depending on whether there is enough money in the pension scheme "pot" to fund the benefits chosen. These are also known as "money purchase" arrangements.

2.10 The benefits available in respect of pensionable service after April 5, 1997 must allow for pensions to increase at least in line with inflation up to 5 per cent each year. In addition the total pension which can be drawn can be increased annually in line with inflation. This costs more than a pension paid at a level rate and so if this option is available more money can be contributed to the pension scheme to fund it. Similarly, when reviewing the level of funding in the scheme, account can be taken of what earnings might grow to when pension age is reached enabling more contributions to be put in the scheme to fund the level of pension this will permit. Often these rules mean that the amount of contributions that can be paid into a pension scheme are greater than employers can afford if maximum pension benefits are to be funded. The benefits actually provided will vary from scheme to scheme and the individual rules of each scheme must be considered. However, if the maximum benefit level has not been reached there is scope for employees to make contributions.

2.11 Although it is a requirement for employers to make contributions to occupational pension schemes, employees can also contribute up to a maximum of 15 per cent of remuneration for each year. The maximum is subject to the earnings cap described above for joiners after July 1989.

2.12 If the scheme rules require the employee to contribute it is known as a contributory scheme. Few, if any, schemes require the employee to contribute as much as 15 per cent of remuneration and some require no contribution at all. It follows that many employees will find that there is scope for them to top up any pension provision made for them by their employer by making their own contributions.

2.13 Great care needs to be taken before making this decision. It is important to appraise exactly what pension benefits are already funded. There is no point in making voluntary contributions if this simply replaces benefits which the employer would otherwise fund.

2.14 There are two options for making contributions. An occupational scheme must operate a facility into which the employee can pay additional voluntary contributions (AVCs). Alternatively the employee can pay his contributions to an insured scheme of his own choosing—a freestanding additional voluntary contribution scheme (FSAVC). Typically the administration costs of the AVC may be met by the employer making it better value for the employee but on the other hand the employee may prefer freedom to choose whichever company he wishes to manage the funds from an investment viewpoint.

2.15 Where the employee has entered into arrangements to pay additional voluntary contributions after April 7, 1987 any pension secured by those contributions cannot be commuted for a lump sum.

2.16 In the event that someone leaves employment before reaching normal retirement date there are four options. The first is that they become entitled to immediate benefits on early retirement, or a deferred benefit is provided for them from the existing scheme. The entitlement to immediate benefits is generally only possible if the individual is aged over 50, and with the consent of the scheme Trustees. The second is that they are entitled to take a transfer value from the existing scheme into either their new employer's scheme or into a personal pension. The third option is that a buyout policy is acquired under which a deferred annuity is purchased from a life insurance company of their own choosing. Finally, where there is less than two years' service, a refund of the employee's own contributions may be possible.

Personal pensions

2.17 The regime for personal pensions was introduced with effect from July 1, 1988. These arrangements are suitable for both the employed and the self-employed, although you cannot make contributions to a personal pension arrangement if you are a member of an occupational pension scheme. For employees a personal pension is therefore an alternative to an occupational retirement benefit scheme, whereas it is the principal option for the self-employed.

2.18 As the name implies, the contract for a personal pension is personal to each individual. If the individual changes jobs the contract will continue to belong to him and depending on his new circumstances can be added to in his new career. Some employers offer group personal pension arrangements where often reduced administration costs can reduce the cost of the contract to the employee. A personal pension contract provides for the following benefits:

- an annuity payable for life starting between the ages of 50 and 75, or on earlier incapacity. Certain people who customarily retire before age 50, such as sportsmen, can draw pension at an earlier age if this is approved by the Inland Revenue;
- a lump sum of 25 per cent of the value of the pension fund;

- an annuity payable for life to a surviving spouse or dependant on the death of the member;
- a death benefit payable on death before age 75. In addition, a refund of contributions made can be paid. This can represent the value of the pension fund, or a refund of contributions with or without interest;
- "income withdrawal" benefits where the purchase of an annuity is deferred. These are explained below.

2.19 Unlike occupational pension schemes, the maximum benefits that can be drawn are limited by the value of the pension fund, not by earnings. Tax limits on the amount that can be contributed to a personal pension are therefore imposed on the level of contributions that can be made in each tax year.

2.20 The maximum contributions that can be paid in each tax year are shown in Table 2.1.

TABLE 2.1

Age at beginning of tax year	% of net relevant earnings
under 36	17.5
36 to 45	20.0
46 to 50	25.0
51 to 55	30.0
56 to 60	35.0
61 or more	40.0

2.21 Of those contributions, 5 per cent can be applied in providing the death benefit. This is usually done through paying premiums on a life assurance policy. For employees any amount of the permitted contribution can be paid by the employer, and the balance by the employee.

2.22 The earnings which count as "net relevant earnings" are emoluments from an office or employment or earnings from a trade, profession or vocation carried on. In the case of an employment, the earnings in question are all those subject to tax including benefits in kind. However, they do not include any earnings arising from shares such as an amount taxed on the exercise of a share option. Nor do they include any amounts which are taxable because they were paid in connection with the termination of the employment. If the employer is an investment company whose income consists wholly or mainly of investments, and the individual controls the company, any remuneration paid to that individual as a director of the company does not count as relevant earnings. Expenses deductible for tax purposes under Schedule E reduce net relevant earnings. Capital allowances also reduce earnings. The self-employed must calculate their taxable profits after deducting payments made for business purposes and these are further reduced by any allowable tax losses in arriving at net relevant earnings. One important exception for those in partnership that need not be deducted is annuities paid to former partners.

2.23 All personal pension contributions are limited by an earnings cap which works by disregarding relevant earnings which exceed the annual limit. That limit is set at £87,600 for 1998/99, and the maximum contribution which can be paid is the percentage (determined according to the age set out in the table above) of the lower of the net relevant earnings for the tax year and the earnings cap.

2.24 Tax relief for contributions made is given as follows:
- contributions paid by employers are not subject to tax on the employee;
- contributions paid by employees are made after deducting relief at the basic rate of tax;
- contributions paid by the self-employed are paid gross;
- relief not given by deduction at source is given by self-assessment through filing a tax return.

Retirement annuities

2.25 Personal pensions replaced retirement annuity contracts and so no new retirement annuity contracts have been issued since July 1, 1988. Pension savings are, however, long-term savings contracts and many of those who had retirement annuity contracts in existence at that time will have chosen to continue them and to add to existing contracts. As a result the regime governing retirement annuities and the interaction with personal pensions needs to be clearly understood.

Like personal pensions, the value of benefits that can be drawn from a retirement annuity contract is limited by the amount which can be paid into the contract in contributions and the value to which they grow over the life of the contract. The maximum contributions that can be paid in each tax year are shown in Table 2.2. **2.26**

TABLE 2.2

Age at beginning of tax year	% of net relevant earnings
under 51	17.5
51 to 55	20.0
56 to 60	22.5
61 or more	27.5

The percentage is applied to net relevant earnings which have broadly the same definition as for personal pensions. Unlike personal pensions, no earnings cap applies and therefore there is no ceiling to the level of earnings used in working out the maximum contribution payable. Like personal pensions, up to 5 per cent of the permitted premium can be used to provide death in service benefits in the form of life assurance or an annuity for a widow/widower or dependant. **2.27**

The benefits which can be drawn from retirement annuities differ in some respect from personal pensions and are: **2.28**

- a pension in the form of an annuity which commences not earlier than age 60 (or earlier on incapacity) and not later than age 75. Like personal pensions, certain occupations where early retirement is normal are allowed to draw pension before age 60;
- a pension for a widow, widower or dependant of not more than the pension payable to the pensioner;

- a tax-free lump sum in commutation of the pension. The maximum must not exceed three times the remaining annuity. Retirement annuity contracts taken out between March 17, 1987 and July 1, 1988 have a cap of £150,000 on the lump sum that can be drawn. As many contracts written at that time were written as clusters of small policies each with a separate £150,000 cap this is rarely a concern in practice;
- in addition to any sum separately insured as a death in service benefit, a return of premiums with or without interest.

2.29 If there is a choice between paying retirement annuities or personal pension contributions, what are the key differences that will influence the decision of which to pick? In summary, the main differences are:

1. *Retirement age.* A retirement annuity policy cannot be drawn until age 60 whereas a personal pension policy can be drawn from age 50. Note that a retirement annuity policy fund can be transferred into a personal pension policy to enable it to be drawn earlier than age 60 but there will be charges and costs involved in doing so. In both cases pension must be drawn no later than age 75.

2. *Allowable contributions.* The percentage of earnings which are payable in contributions differs—see Tables 2.1 and 2.2 above. This may enable more to be paid into one type of contract than another.

3. *Level of earnings.* For those with higher earnings, the earnings cap applicable to personal pensions may be a factor mitigating in favour of retirement annuities. Table 2.3 shows the break-even point in 1998/99.

If a mixture of contributions is paid, the interaction of the rules means that the earnings cap is brought into play for both and this is examined in more depth below.

4. *Lump sum on retiral.* The maximum lump sum that can be withdrawn from a personal pension is 25 per cent of the fund. In the case of a retirement annuity policy the lump sum is restricted to three times the residual annuity. By way of example, on a fund worth £100,000 which is a personal

pension contract, a lump sum of £25,000 could be drawn. Assuming an annuity rate of 8.4 per cent on the same fund, this time as a retirement annuity contract, the lump sum would be £20,127, say just over 20 per cent. This relationship varies considerably according to age and market conditions affecting annuity rates.

5. *Income withdrawals* are not available with retirement annuities.

TABLE 2.3

Age at beginning of tax year	% of relevant earnings payable in retirement annuity premiums	% of relevant earnings payable in personal pension premiums	Break-even point of earnings above which more can be paid in retirement annuity premiums than personal pensions £
35 or less	17.5	17.5	87,600
36 to 45	17.5	20.0	102,617
46 to 50	17.5	25.0	125,142
51 to 55	20.0	30.0	131,400
56 to 60	22.5	35.0	136,267
61 or more	27.5	40.0	127,418

6. *Investment spread.* As only pre-existing retirement annuity contracts can be added to, personal pensions may offer a wider range of investment. This needs to be contrasted with the amount of pension contribution that can be made in each case.

7. *Investment options.* In both cases the main choice will be between a with-profits policy where the policy increases by the addition of bonuses over the life of the policy, and unit-linked policies where the growth in pension fund depends on the value of units at retirement age. There are a wide choice of unit-linked funds available to suit individual investment preferences. Those who have pre-existing retirement annuity policies will be restricted to the choice of investment available on these particular contracts if they add to them.

8. *If contributions are overpaid,* no tax relief is available on the excess. In the case of personal pensions, the Inland Revenue will direct the overpayment to be repaid. In addition, most insurance companies will charge a financial penalty in unscrambling the contract. Strictly speaking retirement annuity funds are taxed on growth where the contribution is excessive but in practice the Inland Revenue do not insist on this except where they identify gross abuse by deliberate overpayment.

Making up for earlier years

2.30 Not everyone pays the maximum contribution possible each tax year under the retirement annuity/personal pension regime. The rules permit contributions paid in the year to be augmented by an amount equal to the unused relief available from earlier years. Unused relief is the difference between the maximum relief that would be available and the contributions actually paid and such relief can be carried forward for a maximum of six years after which it is cancelled on a first-in-first-out basis, *i.e.* relief for an earlier year is cancelled before relief for a later year. In order to make use of unused relief, the maximum permitted contributions for the year must first have been paid.

2.31 In addition to rules permitting unused relief to be carried forward, any contributions paid in one tax year can be treated as paid in the previous tax year, or if there were no relevant earnings in that year, in the tax year before that. For example, any contributions paid in 1998/99 can be treated as paid in 1997/98, provided an election to do so is made by January 31, 2000 and there is the necessary capacity to make the payment in that year.

2.32 The advantage of carrying back a premium to an earlier year is that unused relief brought forward that would expire at the end of that tax year can be utilised. It may also enable the earnings cap to be avoided. In any other circumstance it is unlikely that carrying back premiums will be beneficial. This is because the tax relief due for the contributions is given against the tax payments due for the year in which paid and not by adjustment of the liability for the earlier year.

By way of example, the 1998/99 tax liability will only be reduced by contributions actually paid before April 5, 1999 which are not carried back to an earlier year. Pension premiums paid in 1999/00 which are carried back to 1998/99 are due tax relief which will be calculated by reference to the rates applying in 1998/99, but which will be received by reducing the payment of tax that would otherwise be due to be made on January 31, 2001. It does not reduce payments on account of tax due for 2000/01. **2.33**

A claim to carry back premiums is normally made in the tax return for the year in which the premium is paid but relief can be obtained earlier by making a claim as soon as the premium is paid. The filing deadline for a claim to carry back premiums paid in 1998/99 to 1997/98 is January 31, 2000. **2.34**

Interaction between personal pensions and retirement annuities

The interaction of the rules determining the amount of premiums that can be paid requires the amount of personal pension contributions payable to be restricted by any retirement annuity premiums paid or treated as paid in the same year. Retirement annuity premiums are treated as paid in priority to personal pension premiums. A key point to note is that any personal pension premiums paid will result in the earnings cap applying to the combination of retirement annuity contributions and personal pension contributions together effectively "capping" the former as well. **2.35**

Most difficulty is encountered in applying these rules if a mixture of personal pension contributions and retirement annuity contributions are paid. The following describes a method of working out the limits. **2.36**

2.37   1. Work out the maximum retirement annuity relief available for the tax year in question, using Table 2.4.

TABLE 2.4

Net relevant earnings			£
Maximum relief available A		%	£
Retirement annuity premiums paid in year	£		
Less carried back to earlier year	£		
Add brought back from later year	£		
= Premiums paid and relieved in year B			£
Further relief available = A–B			£
Relief utilised			
Relief for year			£
Add unused relief brought forward—see step 3. below		19 / 19 / 19 / 19 / 19 / 19 /	£ £ £ £ £ £
= Total relief allowed *			

2.38 2. Repeat this exercise for personal pensions, using Table 2.5. If the personal pension premiums paid exceed the relief allowed they must be repaid until the two figures are equal.

TABLE 2.5

Net relevant earnings			£
Earnings cap			£
Relief available		%	£
Less retirement annuity premiums paid and relieved in year (* in Table 2.4)			£
Maximum relief available A			£
Personal pension premiums paid in year	£		
Less carried back to earlier year	£		
Add brought back from later year	£		
= Premiums paid and relieved in year B			£
Further relief available = A–B			£
Relief utilised			
Relief for year			£
Add unused relief brought forward—see step 3. below	19 / 19 / 19 / 19 / 19 / 19 /		£ £ £ £ £ £
= Total relief allowed			

2.39 3. If line B exceeds line A in either table it is necessary to consider if there is unused relief brought forward from earlier years. This can be worked out by repeating the above exercise for each of the last six years and using the results to complete Table 2.6.

TABLE 2.6

Year of assessment	1992/93	1993/94	1994/95	1995/96	1996/97	1997/98	1998/99
Retirement annuities relief							
Max. annual relief Table 2.4—line A							
Less Annual relief utilised Table 2.4—line B							
Less Personal pension contributions paid in year or c/b from later year							
Unused relief available							
Utilised in later year:							
Personal pensions relief							
Max. annual relief							
Less retirement annuities paid and relieved in year							
= Total annual relief allowed							
Adjustment for excess retirement annuity premiums—see note below							
Annual relief utilised Table 2.5—line B							
Unused relief available							
Utilised in later year:							

Exceptionally, retirement annuity premiums paid and relieved in the year will result in the figure of personal pension relief available becoming a negative figure. If this happens unused relief brought forward for personal pensions requires to be cancelled to this extent. However, the negative figure is treated as nil and does not reduce unused relief carried forward in future. **2.40**

What are the disadvantages of making pension contributions?

The main disadvantage is that once you have paid a premium, you cannot recover it until you reach the applicable retirement age. The pension fund is therefore very illiquid and must be regarded as a long-term investment. **2.41**

The second point to remember is that charges are levied on most pension funds and these can erode the investment performance. Charges should be compared carefully in selecting a policy. **2.42**

Pension investment links

In making pension arrangements for your own benefit, as distinct from participating in an employer's scheme, a decision has to be made over what underlying investment link should be chosen. There are two main links that are commonly considered—with-profits policies and unit-linked policies. A with-profits policy works by the insurance company investing the premiums paid. Each year it adds a bonus to the pension fund secured by the investments to represent the accumulated income and capital growth it has earned over the last year. Once added the bonus cannot be removed. For that reason the company will try to smooth out peaks and troughs in its investment performance in declaring bonuses. It will keep some profit back in a good year to enable it to declare a bonus in a bad year when the underlying investments have fallen. **2.43**

A unit-linked policy works by the premiums paid being invested in an underlying fund which is divided into units. If **2.44** the underlying fund grows in value the value of each unit grows—conversely the value can fall if the underlying investment falls. Normally there is a spread between the price at which units are bought and the price at which they are encashed. Charges are also applied to the fund by reducing the number of units held. There is a wide variety of investment links available in most cases, including links to cash and gilts as well as to equities, property and other types of investment.

2.45 Because a unit-linked policy reflects directly the underlying investment performance it is more volatile. For that reason as retirement approaches it is sometimes advisable for the pension-holder to switch the underlying investment to cash and/or gilts to protect against a sudden drop in the underlying fund as the date at which the pension will be drawn approaches. The smoothing effect applied to with-profits policies means that theoretically a unit-linked policy could outperform a with-profits policy if markets are rising but as it can also drop in value the risk is higher. Pension funds should be treated like any other investment and investment links reviewed regularly to check not only if the investment strategy is correct and the investments are in the desired sectors but also that regard is had to the timescale when they must be encashed to provide pension.

Pension alternatives

2.46 Pension policies are just one form of investment and others can equally well be used to save for pension provision. The special tax advantages make pension plans a top consideration but other forms of investment also have tax advantages that enable them to be used, especially those where the fund grows in a tax-free environment.

2.47 Alternatives where the fund is not taxed as it accumulates include personal equity plans, National Savings Certificates and TESSAs. Although contributions into such investments are not tax deductible when paid, the converse is true when withdrawals are made. A pension annuity will suffer tax when paid whereas in the case of the three alternatives mentioned the withdrawal is tax free. The Government has announced its intention to replace personal equity plans and TESSAs with an Independent Savings Account with effect from April 6, 1999. Existing arrangements may be transferred into the new plan.

If you expect your tax rate to be higher when investing, pension contributions are more advantageous from a tax point of view, whereas if you expect your tax rate to be higher in retirement, alternatives may be advantageous. **2.48**

The principal advantage of alternative investments is that they tend to be less illiquid than pensions and you can recover the whole of your capital invested. If you were to die shortly after you started drawing a pension annuity your investment may be partially lost whereas this would not be true of the alternatives mentioned. Consider Tables 2.7 and 2.8, which compare pension investment to non-pension investment assuming the same rate of growth and assuming the alternative is invested in a tax-free environment. **2.49**

In this simple illustration it can be seen that the benefit of tax relief up front means that more can be invested for the same cost and so the fund grows faster to a larger sum. However, the pension annuity when drawn is subject to tax. Withdrawals from other forms of tax-free investment can be withdrawn tax free and so a lower rate of withdrawal is needed to give the same spendable income. As a result the lower fund can meet the same level of income as the pension fund. Of course this is an over-simplified example and many other factors have to be taken into account, not least the rarity of tax-free investment vehicles and the comparative investment returns possible. Table 2.7 also ignores the ability to take a tax-free lump sum and reduced pension. However, the example demonstrates that the ability to provide a pension for those unable to use or top-up approved pension funds is not necessarily a lost cause. When the added liquidity of alternative investment is contrasted with the inability to access pension before retirement age is reached and the fact that it must then be **2.50**

TABLE 2.7

Year	Net premium invested (£)	Tax relief at 23% (£)	Gross premium (£)	Growth at 5% (£)	Cumulative value (£)	Gross pension 5% (£)	Tax on pension (£)	Net receipt (£)
1	7,700	2,300	10,000		10,000			
2	7,700	2,300	10,000	500	20,500			
3	7,700	2,300	10,000	1,025	31,525			
4	7,700	2,300	10,000	1,576	43,101			
5	7,700	2,300	10,000	2,155	55,256			
6	7,700	2,300	10,000	2,763	68,019			
7	7,700	2,300	10,000	3,401	81,420			
8	7,700	2,300	10,000	4,071	95,491			
9	7,700	2,300	10,000	4,775	110,266			
10	7,700	2,300	10,000	5,513	125,779			
11						6,289	1,446	4,843
12						6,289	1,446	4,843

Assumptions:
Investment growth 5% per annum
Tax rate 23%
Pension rate 5% of fund

TABLE 2.8

Year	Annual investment (£)	Tax relief (£)	Growth at 5% (£)	Cumulative fund (£)	Annual withdrawal 5% (£)	Tax at 0% (£)	Net receipt (£)
1	7,700	0		7,700			
2	7,700	0	385	15,785			
3	7,700		789	24,274			
4	7,700		1,214	33,188			
5	7,700		1,659	42,547			
6	7,700		2,128	52,375			
7	7,700		2,619	62,694			
8	7,700		3,135	73,529			
9	7,700		3,676	84,905			
10	7,700		4,245	96,850			
11				96,850	4,843	0	4,843
12				96,850	4,843	0	4,843

used to buy a pension annuity, it can be seen that alternatives can usefully figure in retirement planning.

Unapproved retirement benefit schemes

2.51 Not everyone meets the conditions necessary to join one of the approved pension arrangements described above. In addition, the earnings cap can mean that employees who earn significantly more than this will face a substantial drop in income in retirement unless their pension provision is enhanced. In these circumstances, employers can provide their employees with unapproved pension provision. As pension provision is an important factor in recruiting and retaining employees, especially at senior level, many companies provide such schemes. Where the retirement benefit scheme is unfunded, and the provision amounts to a promise by the employer to make the provision, it is often referred to as an unfunded unapproved retirement benefit scheme or UURB for short. Where the employer sets contributions aside into a trust fund for the employee to provide the benefit it is known as a Funded Unapproved Retirement Benefit scheme or FURB for short.

2.52 Although intended to provide a cushion to the imposition of the earnings cap when introduced, the rules surrounding FURBs and UURBs have been changed several times. Since April 6, 1998, national insurance has been levied on payments into FURBs. Contributions into FURBs are taxed when made but, provided benefits are taken in the form of a lump sum, it is usually possible to draw them tax free. The trust fund itself is liable to tax at the rate of 34 per cent on its income and gains. A main advantage is the flexibility that can be written into the trust fund compared to normal pension schemes, and it would be possible to build up a fund where in the event of the death of the beneficiary before retirement, a tax-free discretionary lump sum would be paid to his heirs. It is usually inadvisable to draw benefits from a FURB in the form of a pension since this will be liable to tax.

Drawing pension

2.53 For members of company occupational pension schemes, there may not be a lot of choice over the timing of drawing pension. The Inland Revenue require there to be actual retirement before the pension is paid although there is nothing to stop the employee taking up new (and different) employment while drawing his pension. The main decision is whether to commute the pension payable for a lump sum. This decision rests entirely on the rate of pension available and the return that can be made from investing the lump sum elsewhere. Remember that a pension annuity is not encashable in future and may lapse on early death, whereas a lump sum is more flexible.

2.54 Holders of retirement annuity policies have more choice. Retirement is not necessary and once the retirement age has been reached the pension benefits can be drawn even if earnings continue. A straightforward choice is to draw pension and again to decide if any pension should be commuted in favour of a lump sum.

2.55 Alternatively, if retirement before age 60 is required or there is a desire to use income withdrawal described below, another option would be to transfer the proceeds of the retirement annuity policies into personal pensions. All the options described for personal pension would then be open.

2.56 A third choice is to consider "staggered vesting" or "phased retirement" as it is also known. Staggered vesting is the name given to the practice of cashing in retirement annuity (or personal pension) policies over a period of time between age 60 and age 75 so as to provide a growing income while preserving pension funds for as long as possible. The advantages of this are:

    (a) the pension fund grows in a beneficial tax environment;
    (b) annuity rates are higher at older ages;
    (c) the remaining funds may be payable free of inheritance tax to family should death occur before the pension is drawn.

2.57 The plan can only be implemented if there is a series of separate contracts that can be cashed in at various times. Since many policies were written as a cluster of separate policies with one company, it is often the case that the scheme can be implemented. Many options are available as to how the plan should be operated, including using tax-free lump sums as income in the early years. The ability to use the plan will depend on total income requirements and income available from other sources such as investment and will not be suitable for everyone. Indeed, it should only be considered if there is a substantial sum held within the pension funds. Table 2.9 provides an illustration.

2.58 Table 2.9 assumes a group of 40 policies worth in total £200,000. The policyholder could encash the entire fund at age 60 and use it to buy an annuity at the rate of 8.4 per cent. After tax at 40 per cent this would give him a level pension for life of £10,080 net of tax. As an alternative, Table 2.9 assumes he encashes only the number of policies shown in the third column each year. On each occasion he commutes his pension for a lump sum of 25 per cent of the fund encashed (column 4) and uses the balance to buy a pension annuity at the rate shown in column 1. This pension, shown in column 5 (net of 40 per cent tax), is added to the pension bought in previous years to give him a cumulative pension shown in column 6. If an assumption is made that the remaining fund grows at 5 per cent per annum it will be worth the figure shown in column 8 at the end of each year. Should the policyholder die, the fund could be paid to his dependants, usually free of inheritance tax. Each year he has spendable income of the lump sum plus the cumulative net pension as shown in column 9, more than his flat-rate pension at age 60. When he reaches age 70 he has encashed his full fund, but his ongoing pension is £15,561 net instead of £10,080. (This example ignores the option of taking a tax-free lump sum and reduced pension at the outset which in practice would feature in this comparison.)

2.59 The strategy is not risk free. Consider the position if annuity rates fall between age 60 and age 70. The advantage of allowing the pension fund to continue to grow is that the

Pensions

TABLE 2.9

Annuity rate (%)	Age	No. of policies encashed	Tax-free cash (£)	New pension net of 40% tax (£)	Cumulative residual net pension (£)	Fund still invested (£)	Fund plus 1 year's growth (£)	Lump sum +pension (£)
							200,000	
8.40	60	8	10,000	1,512	1,512	160,000	168,000	11,512
8.62	61	6	7,875	2,036	3,548	136,500	143,325	11,423
8.84	62	5	6,891	1,827	5,376	115,763	121,551	12,266
9.06	63	5	7,235	1,967	7,342	92,610	97,241	14,578
9.28	64	4	6,078	1,692	9,034	72,930	76,577	15,112
9.50	65	3	4,786	1,364	10,398	57,433	60,304	15,184
9.94	66	3	5,025	1,499	11,897	40,203	42,213	16,922
10.38	67	2	3,518	1,095	12,992	28,142	29,549	16,510
10.82	68	2	3,694	1,199	14,191	14,775	15,513	17,885
11.26	69	1	1,939	655	14,846	7,757	8,144	16,786
11.70	70	1	2,036	715	15,561	0	0	17,597

pension fund is a tax-favoured environment and normally would suffer less tax than an individual would. However, consider the position if the 5 per cent annual growth shown in the illustration had not been achieved. It is also worth bearing in mind that from July 1, 1997 pension funds have been unable to recover the tax credit on dividends which will affect the performance. Nevertheless, if properly applied the strategy is worth considering for larger pension funds.

2.60 Personal pensions offer the same options for drawing pension and again retirement is not a pre-requisite. There is one further option available known as income drawdown. Under this option the decision to buy an annuity can be deferred to age 75 at the latest. Until that time the pension fund supplies the pension which is withdrawn from the fund within limits laid down in the legislation. The earliest date from which income withdrawals can be made is age 50 unless the pension scheme member has become incapable of carrying on his occupation due to infirmity or his occupation is one from which it is customary to retire early, being an occupation listed by the Inland Revenue as falling within this category. The date on which the member first elects to make income withdrawals is known as his pension date. On that date a check is made to see what annuity could have been purchased by him. In each 12-month period starting with that date he must withdraw a minimum of 35 per cent of that annuity and a maximum of 100 per cent. After the first three years a check is again made to see what annuity could be purchased at that time by the remaining fund and that sets new limits within the 35 per cent to 100 per cent overall limit that can be withdrawn for the next three years. This three-year cycle is repeated until the age of 75 is reached when the balance of the fund must be used to buy an annuity. Any lump sum must be taken at the start of an income drawdown plan and is limited to 25 per cent of the fund value at that time.

2.61 *Illustration*:
At age 55, a personal pension fund is worth £100,000. The annuity that could be purchased at that time is 7.6 per cent or £7,600. Instead the member could elect to take a lump sum of £25,000 and an income withdrawal of between £1,995 (35 per

cent of the residual pension) and £5,700 (100 per cent of the residual pension). If the fund grows at 5 per cent per annum and he elects for an income drawdown of £2,000 per annum, after three years the fund would be worth £80,517. If the annuity rate available at that time was 8.5 per cent (because annuity rates had improved and he is three years older) he could either buy a pension of £6,844 or continue with income withdrawal, taking an annual withdrawal of between £2,395 and £6,844. Meanwhile, if he were to die the pension fund remaining would be payable to his heirs usually without incurring inheritance tax and after deducting a tax charge of 35 per cent from the remaining fund.

2.62 Income drawdown is also not without risk. The main risk which has to be assessed is the mortality risk, as if there is a premature death, the capital is preserved for the next generation. However, this is also the reason that annuity income is higher for older lives. To match the income payable by an annuity, the pension fund will normally have to earn a return of capital and income growth greater than the yield available on gilts and fixed interest securities which generally determines annuity rates. In fixing annuity rates actuaries estimate how many annuitants will die earlier than their normal life expectancy. This enables the annuity company to inflate the annuity rate it pays over and above the normal yield earned by the annuity fund. So to match that rate the pension fund has to earn an even greater return than an annuity fund. This difference is referred to as mortality drag.

2.63 As annuity rates increase with older lives the return earned by the pension fund must increase in line with age. This growth rate compared with income from an annuity is referred to as the critical yield. Clearly there is more risk if the critical yield is high and at some point the risk of the pension fund not growing fast enough to match the annuity rate available will make it appropriate to end income withdrawal and buy a pension annuity.

2.64 These investment risks make it very difficult to determine if income withdrawal is beneficial and it must be kept under regular review as investment conditions and annuity rates change. If a fund underperforms or if annuity rates fall, the member could lose out whereas if the investment performance of the pension fund is very good or annuity rates rise income withdrawal will be beneficial. As the risks are quite considerable and it is impossible to predict investment performance with certainty, it is inadvisable for those with small pension funds to consider income withdrawal. By contrast, those with large personal pension funds are likely to find that income withdrawal should be considered, at least in part in determining their strategy for drawing pension.

2.65 Phased retirement and income withdrawal can be combined to good effect. Once an overall strategy for drawing pension has been reached it is possible to consider what options should be applied in buying the pension annuity. Most retirement annuities and personal pensions contain what is known as an open market option, meaning that it is possible not just to buy an annuity from the policy provider but to shop around for the best annuity rates available on the market. These can vary considerably between best and worst provider so a careful review of what is available is essential.

2.66 A number of annuity options are available. A flat-rate annuity will buy a fixed level of pension for life. Alternatively a pension rising at a pre-determined rate per annum or linked to inflation can be purchased. This will be lower in the early years but will provide a growing income in later years. To work out if this is worthwhile involves working out how many years it will take for the break-even point to be reached and then compare this to anticipated life expectancy.

2.67 To provide a widow's pension a joint life pension can be purchased. This will be based on the age of the younger life. To decide if this is worthwhile, an estimate should be made of the spouse's income in retirement after the death of the other spouse. If there is no other source of income or income is likely to be inadequate to maintain the required standard of living a joint pension will be worthwhile.

2.68 Many other options for annuities are available. Special rates are given to those with "impaired lives", *i.e.* ill health which may reduce their life expectancy. With-profits annuities are annuities where income is linked to the stockmarket rather than interest rates. The annuity income rises and falls in line with the stockmarket instead of being fixed. This makes it a riskier investment than a conventional annuity. If there are other dependants, special arrangements may have to be made to provide an income for them on death if permitted by the scheme rules.

State pension

So far, this chapter has looked at private pension provision. However, most British citizens who have spent their working life in the United Kingdom qualify for a state retirement pension. The state pension falls into two parts—a basic pension which everyone who has paid sufficient national insurance contributions qualifies for, and a state earnings related pension (SERPS) which those who have been in employment and paid Class 1 national insurance contributions above the lower earnings limit qualify for depending on their contribution record. Entitlement to state pension is not affected by any other earnings and ends on the death of the pensioner. More details on entitlement to state pension are given in Chapter 6.

2.69

CHAPTER 3

INCOME IN RETIREMENT

Not everyone retires from work at the same age. Some employees find they have no option because their employer sets their retirement age. Others have more control over the age they will retire at. Some people enjoy working and want to carry on for as long as possible, while others want to retire as soon as possible to pursue other vocations or leisure activities which they have not had time for in their working life. **3.1**

Once the timing of retirement has been settled, the next big question that most people ask is "can I afford to retire?" This chapter explains how you can answer that question. **3.2**

Can retirement be afforded?

There are two elements to answering this question. The first is to estimate what income will be in retirement. The second is to predict what expenditure in retirement will be. Provided estimated income exceeds predicted expenditure, retirement can be afforded. It is important to be sure that the comparison is made between income estimated in today's pounds and expenditure estimated in today's pounds. If income falls short of expenditure then there are two options—look to see how income can be increased or look to see how expenditure can be cut. Nowadays people can reasonably expect to live well into their 80s or 90s and an important element of the comparison is to be sure that income will rise during retirement sufficient to meet increasing expenditure due to inflation. If it is clear that full retirement is not financially affordable, partial retirement could be considered. This **3.3** may involve working part-time, or taking up a less demanding job for shorter hours at a lower income. Another alternative is to consider becoming a self-employed consultant if you are a specialist in your field.

Estimating income

3.4 If future income is estimated based on what it will be worth at some future date on retirement, there is a serious danger of being misled as to its spending power. So all figures must be calculated on today's value. It is relatively easy to obtain an estimate of pension income. If an occupational pension scheme is in point, the trustees or their agents can supply an estimate of the pension payable at normal retirement date or on early retirement at some other chosen date. This will be based on length of service at that retirement date and on the size of fund if it is a money purchase arrangement. Be careful that the estimate does not take into account forecast salary increases or that the fund will increase at a certain growth rate until retirement. If these assumptions are made income will be predicted in tomorrow's pounds and the comparison will not be like with like.

3.5 Similarly with retirement annuities and personal pensions, the insurance company will be able to supply an up-to-date estimate of the fund value if it is a with-profits policy. Be careful of estimates that include terminal bonuses. Unlike annual bonuses these are added only when the policy is encashed and are not guaranteed but vary according to the fund's investment performance. It is usually prudent to ignore them for the purpose of any estimate.

3.6 If the policies are unit-linked, prices of the units can usually be obtained from the pages of the *Financial Times* on a daily basis, so that an up-to-date valuation of the policy can be ascertained. Compulsory purchase annuity rates (the rate at which the capital fund is converted into income) are also published regularly in newspapers such as the *Financial Times* or a specific quote can be obtained from an annuity company. Armed with this information it is easy to work out what pension the fund can buy.

Income in Retirement

3.7 To the estimate of pension income must be added any other income, such as bank or building society interest, or investment income from equity investment. Savings that have been put away into TESSAs or PEPs or National Savings may also produce an income in retirement although in some cases an assumption may need to be made about switching them to alternative investments so that income can be drawn and spent.

3.8 Investments which have been made with the objective of saving need to be reviewed and where necessary the investment medium amended to meet needs in retirement. For the purposes of the estimate some assumptions have to be made on what income yield that investment will produce. As an example, income from liquid investments such as cash can be calculated by applying current available interest rates on savings to this sum. Income from quoted investments can be estimated by applying the average stock exchange yield. If the pension forecast is made after allowing for the full tax-free lump sum to be drawn, this lump sum should be added to the capital used in working out investment income.

3.9 A difficulty may arise if assets include a business or shares in an unquoted company, especially if this is likely to be sold on retirement. It may be necessary to estimate what the proceeds of sale might be. In the case of company shares there may be a question mark over whether dividend income might continue to be paid from such sources, especially if there are other shareholders involved. Any estimates in this area should be made on a conservative basis in deciding if retirement is affordable, and in some cases it may be that the decision to retire will be dependent on what the business might realise. If this is the case allowance must be made for tax payable on the sale.

3.10 Care must be taken to ensure that all income is estimated on a gross basis.

Predicting expenditure

3.11 Considering a list of living expenses is a good method of making this prediction. A good starting point is to work out what current levels of expenditure under each heading amount to. A checklist of common items of expenditure is given in Table 3.5 at the end of this chapter, but each individual will have his or her own requirements. Most people can refer back to bills over the last year to work out the figures, but sometimes it may be easier to work out a monthly or quarterly figure and multiply it up to arrive at an annual estimate. Food and drink is an example of this type of expenditure where an estimate will probably have to be made.

3.12 The next stage is to consider how each expenditure heading might change in retirement. For example, some people will find that their commuting costs to work will reduce. On the other hand they may lose the benefit of a company car and have to build in the costs of supplying and running their own car. Another cost that may rise is heating and power if the home will be occupied all day after retirement instead of just part of the time. Clothing requirements may reduce but leisure costs such as club subscriptions and holidays may rise. It is important when carrying out this exercise to be realistic—for example, will socialising after retirement increase or decrease and have costs been adjusted appropriately? Some costs such as pension provision may disappear altogether and many people will have designed their mortgage arrangements so that they too terminate at the same time as retirement.

3.13 If possible divide the costs between those that represent real needs, *e.g.* food and housing costs, and those that represent wants, *e.g.* holidays. If funding retirement is tight it is the latter which should be the focus of any cost cutting. It is a good idea to build in some contingency for extra costs not forecast as well.

3.14 The next heading is income tax. There are two approaches to working this out. If the aim is to calculate the minimum income needed, the expenditure worked out above should be treated as the equivalent of a net income after tax and the tax can be estimated by grossing up the result. If the income figure is reliable an alternative is to work out tax on the gross

Income in Retirement

income and deduct it from income to arrive at net spendable income. In both cases it is best to use current rates of tax and allowances even if these may change before retirement.

Once completed, this exercise will give a good guide as to the level of expenditure required to maintain the current standard of living and the comparison of income and expenditure can begin.   **3.15**

Choosing an annuity pension

As well as helping to determine whether or not retirement is affordable, this exercise also helps in examining options over maximising income. For example, a difficult decision to be made when drawing pension benefits is whether to draw a level pension annuity or to opt for one that escalates in line with inflation. It is worth obtaining quotations for both, and working out how many years the inflation-linked pension must be paid before it catches up with the flat pension. This equates to how many years the pensioner must live before he catches up with the inflation-linked option.   **3.16**

For married couples the exercise can also be repeated in predicting whether there will be sufficient income in retirement following the death of one partner. This may help to establish if it is worth buying a joint annuity to provide a widow's/widower's pension on death. Particularly as more and more couples reach retirement with both having worked sufficiently long to earn pension in their own right, it should no longer be assumed that a pension for the surviving spouse is always the right choice.   **3.17**

Although choosing an inflation-proofed pension may seem attractive, the consequential reduction in the pension that might otherwise be paid may be too large to be justified. Similarly, the drop in value of a joint pension may seem expensive but as an annuity ceases on death it may be essential if family security is to be protected. As more and more people live longer in retirement, the risk of income being insufficient in the future is ever present. It is usually possible to buy a pension annuity where the income is   **3.18** guaranteed for a minimum number of years, five being the most common. Nevertheless, it is impossible to predict when death will occur and for this reason the pension choices available need to be carefully compared before a decision is made. (In the case of a defined benefits scheme these choices are not usually available.)

3.19 Once bought, an annuity cannot be increased. A recent innovation is the availability of an annuity linked to the return on equities. Unlike conventional annuities, this pension can rise with the return on equities, but it can also fall (unlike a conventional annuity) making it a very high-risk option to meet pension requirements. For certain pensioners, despite the risk, it may offer a part in meeting their long-term pension needs.

Topping-up pension income

3.20 Once purchased a pension annuity is totally illiquid and expires on the death of the annuitant. Ideally income provision in retirement will not rest solely on such income but also on the investment return from savings made. If a lump sum has been drawn from a pension arrangement this can also be invested to top-up pension income to the level required for a comfortable retirement. If liquid capital is not available, it may be necessary to consider what sources of capital are available and how they can best be used to generate income. The house is often considered in this respect and this is examined in Chapter 6. It is useful at this stage to draw up a complete list of assets and liabilities. There may be some immediate needs which need to be met such as moving house or buying a car. Funds need to be set aside for these outlays.

3.21 Having established what capital sum is available for investment, the next step is to devise a strategy for investment. Establishing strategy is an essential first step and this can be considered under three headings:
- liquidity
- risk
- taxation.

It may be advisable at this stage to seek advice from a financial adviser on the specific investments that should be chosen. While this chapter does not cover all possible investments, it is intended to outline the main choices available and some of their key features.

Liquidity

The objective of any investment strategy is to produce an overall return in two parts—an income stream and capital growth. There are often unforeseen requirements that crop up and for which liquid funds may be needed quickly, *e.g.* emergency house repairs. For that reason it is always a good idea to set aside some of the available investment funds so that they are immediately available in liquid form in an emergency. There is a tendency to think that these funds should be put in a bank or building society but that is not necessarily the case. For example, an investment in a Government gilt edged security can be sold for cash settlement. This may be more liquid than money in a building society account which, depending on the terms of the account in which it is held, cannot be uplifted for a term of, say, 90 days. Many building societies offer accounts which offer a higher rate of interest the longer you tie up the money—60- or 90-day-notice accounts are common. Some will release money earlier but only if interest is foregone for the notice period. Bear in mind that the liquidity of such accounts carries a price. For example, building society—£10,000 deposit:

3.22

TABLE 3.1

	Interest rate	Annual income
Instant access account	7% gross	£700
90-day account	8% gross	£800
Interest cost on early withdrawal		(£200)
Total		£600

Risk

Risk is a very subjective issue and various categories of investment can span different risk sectors. Low-risk investments are ones that are guaranteed by the Government or

3.23

other agencies. High-risk investments are ones where your capital is at risk. Unfortunately, the total return of both income and capital growth on low-risk investment is often considerably less than that usually available on high-risk investments (although tax concessions can bridge the gap) so there is usually a balance to be struck. Undernoted are a number of common investment categories with reasons why they are graded low, medium or high risk. The investments covered are not all that are available but represent the main choices available.

Bank/building society (low risk)

(a) Security

3.24 These rank as a very low-risk investment from the viewpoint of security of capital provided investment is limited to amounts covered by the depositor protection schemes. In the case of a sterling bank account or a United Kingdom building society 90 per cent of the investment up to the first £20,000 invested is covered in the event of a bank or building society failure.

3.25 To minimise the risk, an investment of more than £20,000 should be spread over more than one bank or building society. Remember, however, that the higher the deposit the higher the rate of interest that is usually paid.

(b) Interest rates

3.26 It is relatively easy to establish comparative interest rates from sources such as *Money Facts*,[1] the financial press, or the banks and building societies themselves. However, interest rates will vary even within one organisation according to two criteria in particular:
- size of deposit
- access to funds/notice period of withdrawal.

In comparing interest rates make sure that the gross composite annual rate (gross CAR) is used which takes into account the compounding effect of the date of payment of interest.

[1] Published by Moneyfacts Publications.

Beware also accounts becoming obsolete. Building societies frequently change the terms of accounts on offer and when they do so they may reduce interest rates dramatically on the discontinued account, often with minimal advertisement of the change. It is important to ensure that the accounts are kept under regular review and if appropriate the account closed and switched to a new account offering better terms. 3.27

(c) TESSAs (tax exempt special savings accounts)

The advantage of this type of account over a normal bank account is twofold: 3.28

- interest is not liable to income tax
- higher interest rates may be available on such accounts.

The account is only available to an individual aged 18 or over and cannot be a joint account. The conditions attaching to it must be satisfied for a period of five years ending with the anniversary of the day it was opened or until the account holder dies if earlier.

New TESSA accounts can only be opened up to April 5, 1999 but additions can be made thereafter to existing accounts for the full five-year life of the account. The maximum that can be deposited in an account over the five-year period is £9,000 but this can only be subscribed by depositing a maximum of £3,000 during the first 12 months the account is opened and a maximum of £1,800 in each succeeding 12-month period. If the full £3,000 is subscribed in year one the maximum that can be deposited in year five is, therefore, £600. 3.29

The account cannot be connected to another account but the Inland Revenue do not apply this rule to what is known as "feeder" accounts. A feeder account is an ordinary account on which interest is taxable and from which automatic maximum transfers are made to the TESSA account on each anniversary. These accounts tend to be offered at very attractive interest rates. TESSA accounts cannot be assigned or used as security for a loan. 3.30

3.31 At the end of a five-year period the TESSA matures and you have the option to withdraw your capital plus any accumulated interest or to roll over the capital into a new independent savings account which is described below. Neither subscriptions to TESSAs nor any capital transferred on maturity will affect the amount that can be subscribed to the new independent savings account.

3.32 The objection most often put forward against opening a TESSA account is that the funds are tied up for a five-year period and the interest is not available to the investor during this period—both are incorrect.

3.33 A withdrawal from the account will only cause it to lose its tax-exempt status. Thus, in an emergency the funds can still be accessed but the interest will suffer tax in the year in which it ceased to qualify as a TESSA.

3.34 Interest withdrawals will not cause the account to lose its TESSA status provided they do not exceed the cumulative interest paid to date net of the basic rate of tax that applied when the interest was paid. So the net equivalent interest can be withdrawn *provided* that the terms of the account offered by the particular bank or building society permits this. A TESSA account can also be switched from one bank or building society to another (which enables advantage to be taken of better interest rates) but again close attention needs to be paid to the particular terms attaching to the account as some banks or building societies apply a penalty. It follows that when opening a TESSA regard should be had not just to comparative interest rates but also to the conditions relating to withdrawals and switching.

Individual savings accounts (ISAs)

3.35 This new form of investment will be a stand-alone savings product guaranteed to run for at least 10 years starting on April 6, 1999. The regulations governing these accounts were laid before Parliament on July 31, 1998, and as no accounts are available at the time of writing there is still some uncertainty as to how the accounts will operate in practice.

There will be no lifetime limit to the maximum amount that can be invested in an ISA. Cash (including National Savings), life insurance and stocks and shares (including gilts bought with at least five years to go to maturity) will all be included in the components of an ISA. The account will have an annual subscription limit of £5,000 of which no more than £1,000 can go into cash and £1,000 into life insurance. In 1999/2000 only, the annual limit will be £7,000, of which no more than £3,000 can go into cash and £1,000 into life insurance. Interest, dividends and capital gains on assets held within the account will not be liable to income or capital gains tax, with the exception of interest on cash held within the stocks and shares or insurance elements, where tax of 20 per cent will be deducted at source. Although tax credits on dividends will not be refundable after April 6, 1999 normally, a 10 per cent tax credit will be payable on dividends from United Kingdom equities held in ISAs during the five-year period to April 2004.

3.36 It is proposed that there will be three investment routes, the "maxi" route and the "mini" route and a TESSA only account into which the capital from matured TESSAs can be transferred. In the "maxi" route, the investor will subscribe to only one account manager in each tax year but will be able to split his subscription between the component elements as he wishes subject to the maximum levels for cash and life insurance. Under the "mini" route the investor can subscribe separately to different managers for each component. There will be a limit of £3,000 for the stocks and shares component with no opportunity to transfer unused subscription moneys from the other components. There will be no minimum subscription or minimum period for which the ISA must be held but there is no scope to transfer funds between components.

3.37 It will be possible to transfer capital from a TESSA within six months of its maturity. In the case of TESSAs maturing between January 6, 1999 and April 5, 1999, the investor can transfer the capital directly into an ISA after April 5, 1999. This will only be transferable into the cash component and will not count against the annual subscription. Details of how this savings account will operate, which companies will offer it and how it will work in practice remain to be seen. The Government hopes it will be a value-for-money investment and to help achieve this they are consulting with the industry on setting benchmarks or standards on cost, access and terms (CAT standards). The CAT standards will cover interest rates on the cash element, charges on the other elements, minimum subscriptions and premiums, penalties for withdrawals, surrender values and single pricing. If introduced, providers of ISAs will have to state if their product does not meet the required CAT standard. These standards do not determine the risk factor of an ISA and its risk status will depend on what is comprised in it. As tax-free forms of investment are rare, it is likely to be an important savings medium.

National Savings products (low risk)

3.38 National Savings products are investments which are offered, and managed, by the Department of National Savings on behalf of the United Kingdom Government who underwrite the investment. From a security viewpoint they are, therefore, very low risk. The issues are withdrawn and replaced regularly as interest rates change and the following information relates to the issues available at the time of writing. Details on current and subsequent issues can be obtained from post offices or by contacting National Savings either by post or on its helpline on 0645 645 000.

(a) 13th issue index-linked National Savings certificates

3.39 Funds invested in this issue increase in line with the movement in the retail prices index, together with a fixed bonus as shown in Table 3.2. If the certificates are held for five years, these rates give a return equal to 2.25 per cent per annum compound on top of the index linking.

3.40 The increase in the value at the end of each year is compounded and the return is tax free. The maximum holding is £10,000 (minimum £100).

TABLE 3.2

Minimum period held	Increase in value
One year	RPI plus 1.0%
Two years	RPI plus 1.2%
Three years	RPI plus 1.6%
Four years	RPI plus 2.6%
Five years	RPI plus 4.9%

To work out the yield available consider the current level of inflation. If, for example, inflation runs at an average of 4 per cent over five years the net return would be 6.25 per cent. In the case of a taxpayer who pays tax at 20 per cent this equates to a gross yield of 7.8125 per cent and in the case of a 40 per cent taxpayer, 10.416 per cent. The problem in evaluating this issue is that inflation is an unknown quantity over a five-year period. However, the inflation-linked return ensures that this investment will retain its value to this extent over the next five years. As a long-term investment this is competitive, although early encashment would result in a substantial reduction in return. **3.41**

(b) Ordinary issue certificates

By comparison with the index-linked issue, ordinary saving certificates offer a fixed return over a five-year period. The rate of return rises on each anniversary of the investment with the highest return coming in the last years to produce a lower overall average. This inevitably means the return in the earlier years can be low and hence this should in general be regarded as a five-year investment. Although in theory these certificates do not provide any income, a regular encashment programme can be undertaken on each issue, which can provide quite a competitive annual tax-free income. An illustration of how an income can be drawn is shown in Table 3.3, based on £10,000 invested in the 46th issue. "Income" drawn by this method would not count in determining the income limit for age allowance for income tax purposes. **3.42**

62   Money Matters

TABLE 3.3

End of year	£100 certificates encashed	Value of certificates encashed (£)	Certificates remaining	Value (£)
1	4	414.40	96	9,945.60
2	4	430.16	92	9,893.68
3	4	449.08	88	9,879.76
4	4	472.44	84	9,921.24
5	4	505.68	80	10,113.60

(c) First option bonds

3.43 This is a National Savings product aimed at basic rate taxpayers. Unusually for National Savings, tax is deducted at source. The minimum investment is £1,000 and the maximum is £250,000. By investing you commit to retain your holding for a 12-month period and the interest rate payable is reviewed every 12 months. As you tie into that interest rate for 12 months at a time, the bond is attractive if interest rates are expected to fall but less so if economic trends suggest a rise. The current first year fixed rate is 6.75 per cent gross (5.4 per cent net). Bonds of £20,000 or more held to the first anniversary earn a bonus making the interest 7 per cent gross (5.6 per cent net). Bonds can be cashed at each anniversary but no interest is earned if encashed before the first anniversary. If encashed inbetween anniversaries, interest calculated on a daily basis at half the fixed rate applying since the last anniversary is added to the value at the last anniversary. Part of a bond can be encashed so that the interest earned can be withdrawn by making an annual partial encashment. Interest is paid net of tax at the lower rate of 20 per cent.

(d) Income bonds

3.44 These pay a fairly high rate of interest gross monthly (currently 7 per cent gross or 7.25 per cent on investments over £25,000). They are useful if high income is needed or for those who do not pay income tax (because of an excess of allowances for example) as there is no need to recover tax deducted at source. Three months' notice is required to uplift the bonds and there is a minimum investment of £2,000 and a maximum of £250,000.

(e) Pensioners' Guaranteed Income Bond

3.45 This bond is available for people aged 60 and over. Between £500 and £50,000 can be invested for a five-year term. The rate of interest payable on the 5th series bond is 6.10 per cent gross. Interest is paid gross each month but the income is liable to tax. As the interest is taxable care needs to be taken that sufficient funds are reserved from the income to meet any tax liability when due. Access to funds within the five-year term can be obtained on giving 60 days' notice during which no interest is paid. Immediate access is available but subject to 90 days' loss of interest.

(f) Capital bonds

3.46 These are aimed at non-taxpayers who do not require income—a rare combination. The interest is taxable on an annual basis although it is not paid out until the end of five years when it is paid gross. Taxpayers must, therefore, fund the tax liability on the bonds out of other sources, which is why they are unsuitable for taxpaying investors. The advantage is that you lock into an interest rate for five years but the return is higher in the later years and fairly low in the early years, penalising early encashment. For example, Series L bonds pay 4.4 per cent in year one rising to 8.46 per cent at the end of year five, an average of 6 per cent.

Government securities (low risk)

3.47 Gilts are bonds issued by the United Kingdom Government. Like National Savings they are used to bridge the gap between what the Government receives in income from taxation and what it spends on health, education, defence, etc. Most gilts pay a fixed rate of interest with the exception of indexed linked issues where the income rises in line with the retail prices index.

3.48 Most gilts have a face value of 100 pence and will be repaid at that level. Again indexed linked are an exception; their repayment value is linked to the RPI. If you buy a gilt priced at under 100 and hold it until it is repaid on its predetermined maturity date, you will be certain of a capital gain. Profits on gilts are exempt from capital gains tax but income tax is payable on the interest paid. Interest is paid gross unless the investor opts for tax to be deducted at source.

3.49 If held to maturity, a gilt trading at below 100 will offer a capital gain. If a gilt trading above 100 is purchased, a capital loss will arise when the gilt matures, *i.e.* capital may be converted into income.

3.50 Gilts are bought and sold on the Stock Exchange like shares and their prices go up and down. Prospective buyers do not, therefore, have to wait for a new issue to acquire them or to wait until the maturity date to dispose of them. Various factors affect prices and the most important is the general level of interest rates. As well as buying through a stockbroker new issue gilts can be bought by direct application to the Bank of England. Announcements of a new issue can be found in the newspapers from time to time, usually on a Sunday or Monday. The Stock Register allows persons to buy and sell gilts which are already in issue without going through a stockbroker. Since July 20, 1998 the Bank of England has run the Register whereas formerly National Savings ran it. Not all gilts are available on the Stock Register and a list of those currently available can be obtained on request.

3.51 The advantage of buying direct from the Stock Register is that commissions tend to be lower, especially for smaller purchases. Commissions start at 0.7 per cent with a minimum of £12.50 on purchases and no minimum on sales. On transactions worth above £5,000 the commission is £35 plus 0.375 per cent of the excess over £5,000. No advice is provided on which issue to buy. Gilts are suitable investments for people looking for a fixed and secure income but you can only be sure how much capital you will get back if you hold them to redemption. Higher rate taxpayers and people who pay capital gains tax can benefit from low coupon gilts if their price is below the nominal value because any capital gain will be tax free. Few low coupon gilts are currently available.

If gilts are sold together with the right to the next interest payment (cum dividend) part of the price received is accrued interest and tax is payable on this amount. If the gilt is sold during the ex-dividend period tax relief can be claimed for the amount of accrued interest deducted from the price. For buyers of gilts the position is reversed. Tax relief is given for the amount of accrued interest added to the price during the cum dividend period and tax is paid on the accrued interest deducted during the ex-dividend period. If the total nominal value of all the gilts held by each individual is £5,000 or less then the accrued interest scheme does not apply. **3.52**

One particular form of gilt, which is less well understood, is the index-linked gilt. The repayment value of an indexed gilt is linked to the retail prices index. In addition, there is a small coupon (usually 2 per cent or 2.5 per cent) which increases in line with inflation each year. What is often less clearly understood is that the retail prices index used in the calculation is the index eight months before issue and maturity. Thus if held to maturity the return cannot be guaranteed to match inflation because of the eight-month time lag. Similarly, if sold before maturity market influences on the price may prevent the stock from matching inflation exactly. Quoted yields for the index-linked gilts appearing in the *Financial Times* show the real yield assuming inflation of both 5 per cent and 10 per cent. **3.53**

Building society permanent interest bearing shares (PIBS) (medium risk)

These are a comparatively new style of investment first launched in the summer of 1991 and are comparable to gilts. They are traded on the Stock Market and purchased through stockbrokers subject to a minimum investment usually of £1,000 nominal value. They are essentially loans to building societies on which a fixed rate of interest is paid twice a year, **3.54** but unlike gilts they are irredeemable. Their value, therefore, depends on the price at which they are traded in the market. Interest is paid subject to deduction of income tax at the lower rate. Dealing costs include stockbrokers' commissions at rates comparable to gilt dealings and a buy/sell spread of between 0.5 per cent and 0.75 per cent. They are a form of qualifying corporate bond and hence any capital gain is exempt from capital gains tax. The yield in these investments will be slightly higher than gilts because the risk is higher. If the building society were to collapse the PIBS holder would rank behind other depositors and creditors and if an interest payment was missed because the building society was in trouble it would be under no obligation to make it up. Additionally, PIBS are less liquid than gilts. They are, however, suitable for use in providing a regular fixed income at modest risk.

Other qualifying corporate bonds (medium to high risk)

3.55 A qualifying corporate bond is a security, the debt on which represents a normal commercial loan which is expressed in sterling and in respect of which no provision is made for the conversion into or redemption in a currency other than sterling. The securities may be quoted or unquoted and are issued by both quoted and unquoted companies. Risk accordingly varies depending on the issuing company.

3.56 The main feature of a qualifying corporate bond as far as an investor is concerned is that any gain is exempt from capital gains tax. The corollary is that it cannot give rise to an allowable loss. Income is taxable as it arises.

Purchased life annuities (low risk)

3.57 Annuities are issued by insurance companies and in exchange for payment of a lump sum, the capital invested purchases a fixed return in the form of income over the lifetime of the investor or, in the case of a temporary annuity, over a fixed number of years. At the end of the annuity period the capital is not returned. The annuity rate varies and tends to move in line with movements in gilt yields.

Unlike pension annuities, a purchased life annuity falls into two parts calculated actuarially over the life of the annuitant. The first part, the capital element, is not taxable, and the older the age of the annuitant at date of purchase, the greater is this element. The second part, the income element, will have income tax deducted at source and this is refundable if tax is not due. It is normal for the annuity to be guaranteed for a fixed number of years so that in the event of early death a reasonable recovery of capital invested is made. However, the nature of an annuity makes it unsuitable for those who have dependants (unless structured on joint lives or linked with an endowment assurance policy). A joint life annuity will normally be based on the life expectancy of the younger or better health life. The biggest danger with a life annuity is inflation, which can erode the value of the fixed income with no means of accessing capital to correct the position. For this reason annuities tend to be of interest only to older lives except to meet very specific requirements.

Investment bonds (medium to high risk)

These are single premium life assurance policies. Their return depends on the underlying performance of the insurance fund they are linked to—in this they are similar to unit trusts in that the insurance company will select and manage the underlying investments. The main feature of the bonds is their tax treatment, which can be useful as a planning tool. As a non-qualifying life policy the proceeds of a bond less the premiums paid are subject to tax at basic and higher rates. However, the lower rate liability is deemed to have been satisfied by deduction of tax at source (non-refundable to non-taxpayers). A higher rate taxpayer is liable to tax at the difference between the higher and lower rates on the gain although in determining liability the gain is divided over the number of years the policy has run in order to determine the tax rate applicable. Prior to maturity the investor may draw up to 5 per cent of the initial premium per annum (cumulated if not drawn) without crystallising a tax charge. This is often described as a tax-free withdrawal but for tax purposes it is deducted from the initial premium increasing the gain in the policy when it is finally encashed, so "tax deferred" is a better

3.58

description. A basic rate taxpayer can take higher withdrawals without having to pay any further tax, provided the level does not breach the higher rate tax band. Although insurance companies may actively encourage such withdrawals in their selling literature, problems can and do arise if the growth in the bond fails to keep pace with the withdrawals made so that effectively the bondholder is living on capital. There is no general relief against other gains if a loss is suffered on a bond. On final encashment, a deficiency can be deducted from total income for the purpose of higher rate tax only (provided it does not exceed previous gains on earlier chargeable events). The bonds can, however, be useful where income is needed which is not liable to tax. In particular, this can be used to preserve entitlement to age allowance.

Equity investment (high risk)

3.59 Investment in stocks and shares quoted on the stock market is subject to the volatility of the stock exchange. Historically, rising dividends have resulted in investment in the stock exchange providing a long-term hedge against inflation and falling interest rates which fixed interest investments cannot match. However, equities can fall in value as well as rise, and company dividends can be cut without warning. For that reason this form of investment is conventionally described as high risk. The risk can be reduced by spreading investment over more than one shareholding. Income from equities is received in the form of dividends. These can take a variety of forms (ordinary dividend, preference dividend, foreign income dividend, stock dividend, etc.) but typically dividends carry a tax credit of 20 per cent leaving only higher rate tax if any to be paid on the sum of the dividend plus tax credit. Unfortunately after April 6, 1999 this tax credit drops to 10 per cent and will cease to be recoverable for those whose tax liability is lower than the tax credits suffered. Any gains on selling shares are subject to capital gains tax subject to an annual exemption per individual.

Personal equity plans (PEPs)

3.60 A PEP is a means of holding stocks and shares, unit trusts or investment trusts within a vehicle which attracts tax

Income in Retirement 69

advantages. Investments held within a PEP do not suffer income tax or capital gains tax but nor are capital losses allowable. Currently, the annual amount that can be invested in a general PEP is £6,000 per annum and a further £3,000 can be put into a single company PEP each year. The ability to subscribe to a PEP is withdrawn after April 5, 1999. PEPs held on April 5, 1999 will be able to continue under the current rules, outside the new individual savings account. They will receive tax relief on the same basis as the new individual savings account, including for five years the 10 per cent tax credit on United Kingdom equities. No further subscriptions will be allowed after April 5, 1999. The value of PEP holdings will not affect the amount that can be subscribed to the new individual savings account.

Principal PEP rules 1998/99

These are as follows: **3.61**

- investor must be aged 18 or over;
- investor must be resident or ordinarily resident in the United Kingdom;
- only one plan can be subscribed to per annum (other than a single-company PEP);
- investments are limited broadly to shares in U.K. companies or qualifying E.C. shares or to investment trusts or authorised unit trusts which themselves hold 50 per cent of their investments in U.K. equities and comparable E.C. companies. Up to £1,500 can be held in investment trusts or unit trusts which do not meet this condition. Alternatively "corporate bond" PEPs may hold investments in qualifying fixed interest securities;
- the PEP must be managed by a fund manager;
- the plan must be designated, and cash held, in sterling only;
- dividends may be reinvested or distributed.

A single-company PEP is one where investment is restricted to only one company at a time and consequently this is usually higher risk than a managed general PEP where there is a spread of investment. **3.62**

3.63 PEPs take three forms:

- discretionay or managed PEPs involving common management of investments by a plan manager who takes decisions on the composition of the portfolio;
- non-discretionary or self-select PEPs where the plan manager simply executes instructions and the choice of investment lies with the investor;
- investment trust or unit-trust-linked PEPs.

Apart from investment selection the main difference lies in the charges. Typically, charges for self-select PEPs are less than those for managed PEPs but charging structures vary dramatically and should be considered before selecting a PEP.

3.64 In deciding if a PEP is appropriate (and if so, what type), compare:

(a) the yield from the investments chosen—the tax recovery will boost this;
(b) the effect of charges—someone who buys unit trusts or has a managed portfolio will pay charges anyway, but someone who manages their own portfolio will find these an extra expense;
(c) the effect of the individual's income tax rate—the tax saving made by a higher rate taxpayer may exceed any costs.

3.65 In addition, the capital gains tax exemption must be considered—if the annual capital gains tax exemption is used regularly, the PEP represents further relief. If it is not, the decision to hold assets in a PEP may be more marginal. If investments are managed on a personal basis by the investor, the PEP is likely to be beneficial if higher rate tax is paid, but of a fairly marginal benefit if it is not. However, tax-free forms of investment are rare and as the fund in your PEP increases in capital value through growth and further annual subscriptions, the benefit can increase with the effluxion of time.

Income in Retirement 71

Collective investments

Equity investment is usually classified as high risk because of the potential volatile performance of any one share quoted on the stock market. Having a spread of investments can reduce the risk and one way of obtaining a spread is to invest in either unit trusts, investment trusts or open-ended investment companies which are themselves holders of an underlying portfolio of stocks and shares. **3.66**

Main features of unit trusts

A unit trust is an investment fund with an unspecified capital established by a trust deed. In trust terms the "beneficiaries" of a unit trust are the unit holders who share in both income and capital on the basis of the number of units held. A unit trust is, therefore, constituted by trust deed and governed by trust law. A trustee is appointed (typically a large bank or insurance company) who is responsible for safeguarding the trust's assets and looking after the interests of the unit holders. A manager is also appointed to carry out the day-to-day management of the unit trust and it is the manager who is usually responsible for investment decisions. **3.67**

Amongst other things the trust deed of a unit trust will include provisions concerning the trust investment objectives, the manager's permitted charges, other charges and the extent of its investment and borrowing powers. A unit trust is an open-ended fund which means it expands or contracts in size depending on the level of demand from investors. This means that as more investors wish to invest, more units will be issued to accommodate them and the funds invested will go to increase the fund size. If, on the contrary, unit holders are selling their units (which cannot be resold to existing unit holders or new investors) the trustee will sell investments out of the underlying fund to provide cash to buy back the units via the manager and the fund size will decrease. The price of units in the unit trust is determined directly by changes in the value of stocks and shares held by the trust. There is only one portfolio of underlying **3.68** assets, which is equally shared by all unit holders. The price at which units are bought and sold is subject to a bid/offer spread (usually 6 per cent) and the management will also charge an annual management fee. Typically there are two different types of units available to unit holders—income units where income is paid out to unit holders in cash or is used to purchase additional units, and accumulation units where income is rolled up into the existing units held, thereby increasing the value per unit. The scope of the fund managers to invest unit trusts is more tightly regulated than investment trusts and hence investors who want exposure to more unusual markets may find that they cannot achieve this through unit trusts. Unit trusts cannot borrow and hence cannot gear up the investment portfolio. An authorised unit trust does not suffer tax on its capital gains but income and gains made on the disposal of the units are taxed in the hands of the investor with a tax credit attaching to income paid. There are more unit trusts available than investment trusts and their performance has been extremely varied. This can make the choice extremely difficult and professional advice is recommended.

Main features of investment trusts

3.69 Investment trusts, on the other hand, contrary to what their name implies, are not trusts at all. They are quoted companies subject to Stock Exchange and Financial Services Act requirements. The company is a limited liability company, which is regulated by its memorandum and articles of association. Unlike a unit trust an investment trust is not subject to DTI rules or SIB approval. An investment trust is close-ended. The size of the company's initial share capital is determined by the amount of share capital raised when it is floated on the stock market. Once investors have subscribed for shares they can only recoup their investment by buying and selling on the market. There is no manager to buy and sell shares as there is with a unit trust. The price of investment trust shares is influenced not only by changes in the net asset value of the company's underlying investment portfolio but also by investors' supply and demand for shares. The scope of investment for investment trusts is less regulated than a unit trust and hence there is a wider choice of markets in which it can invest. It can borrow and this enables it to gear up to increase its investments. This can be an advantage in enabling it to buy shares at the right time and a disadvantage if share prices drop as it makes the investment more volatile.

3.70 An investment trust can issue various types of shares and stock, etc., and some investment trusts have two or more classes of share which involve the separation of ownership of income and capital. These are commonly referred to as split capital investment trusts. Different classes of share can involve more or less risk and specialised advice is essential when purchasing or selling such investments.

3.71 Investment trusts have a trade association—the Association of Investment Trust Companies—and there are currently more than 200 investment trust companies listed on the Stock Exchange. Like unit trusts the extensive choice can make it just as difficult to choose a suitable investment trust as it is to buy individual stocks and shares. Some specialise by geographical division, *e.g.* Europe, North America and some by industry sector. Others have a policy of high income and some capital growth. Others operate within ethical guidelines. There are no charges or bid/offer spreads involved in buying investment trust shares although there is a stockbroker's commission in the normal way. Dividends from an investment trust carry a tax credit and like unit trusts an investment trust is itself exempt from tax and capital gains. The shareholder is, however, taxable in the normal way in both cases.

3.72 In terms of past performance there is little to choose between investment trusts and unit trusts and tables show that the best and worst performers are very comparable. Information readily available on investment trusts usually includes the net asset value. Sometimes an investment trust trades at a discount to net asset value mainly because there are more sellers than buyers of the shares. If demand is greater than the number of shares available the shares trade at a premium to net assets. This increases risk as the discount/premium can widen/narrow if demand falls for the shares.

Main features of Open-ended Investment Companies (OEICs)

3.73 European investors have difficulty with the concept of a trust, and so to introduce a collective investment vehicle to the United Kingdom that is equivalent to a unit trust but attractive to foreign investors the decision was made in 1993 to introduce OEICs. The rules that govern OEICs were only finalised in 1997 and a number of existing unit trusts have converted or are in the course of converting to OEICs. It is expected that the number of OEICs available will continue to grow steadily. An OEIC is constituted as a company but it is open-ended as its shares are continuously created or redeemed according to demand in the same way as units in a unit trust. Most OEICs will have an umbrella structure with a range of sub-funds which investors can switch between. More than one class of share, each with its own charging structure, can be issued giving it similarities to split capital investment trusts. Unlike unit trusts there is no bid/offer spread and shares are bought and sold at a single mid-price, based on the value of the fund divided by the number of shares in issue each day, referred to as the net asset value. An initial fee is added to the net asset value price which is intended to make charges transparent.

Taxation

3.74 The tax position of each investment is important because it could affect the choice of investment which is best for each individual. Ideally, husband and wife should have sufficient income to use their personal allowances, lower rate band and basic rate band each. It may be appropriate to choose investments that do not yield taxable income, *e.g.* National Savings certificates, TESSAs or PEPs for those that fall into the higher rate tax bracket and also for those whose income level enables them to qualify for age allowance. Dividends and interest are taxable at the rate of 20 per cent in 1998/99 while higher rate taxpayers pay 40 per cent. After April 6, 1999, the income tax charge on dividends falls to 10 per cent for those who are not higher rate taxpayers but a refund of the tax credit of 10 per cent ceases to be available for non-taxpayers. It may be more appropriate for those affected to switch to fixed interest investments although the effect on capital growth needs to be considered as well. Higher rate taxpayers are charged at the rate of 32.5 per cent on dividends plus tax credits after April 6, 1999. Net of the tax credit of 10 per cent, this leaves them in the same net position as in 1998/99 when they are charged 40 per cent (less a tax credit of 20 per cent).

As well as the income tax position it must be remembered that capital gains tax is payable on chargeable gains. If capital growth can be realised tax free within the annual exemption this may be a better option than income producing investments. Unfortunately it is difficult to find investments where the capital return is guaranteed.   **3.75**

Capital gains tax

The capital gains tax system is complex. The tax rate that applies to gains is the rate that would apply if the taxable gains were the top slice of income, so the rate is determined by the marginal income tax rate and is a maximum of 40 per cent. The basic gain on the disposal of any asset is the difference between the cost of an asset and its disposal value. The chargeable gain is further reduced by an allowance for inflation known as the indexation allowance. The allowance is calculated by reference to the growth in the retail price index between the date of acquisition of the asset (subject to a starting date no earlier than March 1982), and the date of disposal. However, no indexation is allowed for periods after April 6, 1998.   **3.76**

In the case of shares, or other similar assets that cannot be individually identified, special rules apply to work out which assets have been disposed of if the whole holding is not sold. These are known as the identification rules. The rules are different for companies and the undernoted rules apply to individuals only. Each disposal is taken in turn, earliest first; that disposal is identified first with any shares acquired in the period of 30 days after the disposal. This stops a practice known as "bed & breakfasting" whereby shares could be sold on one day and bought back the next   **3.77** deliberately to crystallise either a gain or a loss. Shares acquired on the same day are also matched with a disposal. Once these transactions are eliminated, shares disposed of are matched with earlier acquisitions on a last in first out basis, *i.e.* later acquisitions first. Acquisitions fall into three groups—those arising after April 6, 1998, which are identified first, then those held at April 6, 1998 and finally those held at April 6, 1982. Shares held at April 6, 1998 are indexed as described above and treated as one single pooled holding. Shares held at April 6, 1982 are not included in this pool and are identified after the April 6, 1998 pool has been exhausted. If shares are received under a reorganisation of a company's share capital, such as a bonus issue or rights issue, they are generally treated as being acquired at the same time as the original shareholding. Indexation on any additional cost paid on a rights issue runs only from the date paid, however.

3.78 Once the shares, or other assets being disposed of, have been identified, a relief known as taper relief is given in arriving at the tax payable on the gain. The amount of the relief varies according to whether it is a business asset or a non-business asset, and the length of time it has been held. A non-business asset must be held for a minimum period of three years after April 6, 1998 before the gain is tapered. A business asset is tapered after it has been held for one whole year after April 6, 1998. In both cases, for assets held at March 17, 1998 the asset is treated as having been held after April 6, 1998 for one extra year and this means that business assets held at April 6, 1998 qualify for taper relief in 1998/99. Table 3.4 sets out the scale for tapering relief.

3.79 Once the taxable amount of each asset disposed of has been calculated, the gains are added together. In each tax year a further exemption is given for a fixed amount of gains known as the annual exemption. In 1998/99 the exemption is £6,800.

3.80 Losses are calculated in the same way as gains except that indexation cannot create a loss. Losses are first offset against all gains within the year. Unused losses can be carried forward to the next tax year. Where the losses are carried forward the amount used up is generally restricted to the amount required to reduce the net gains of the year to the amount of the annual exemption.

TABLE 3.4

Gain on disposals of business assets		Gain on disposals of non-business assets	
No. of whole years in qualifying holding period	Percentage of gain chargeable	No. of whole years in qualifying holding period	Percentage of gain chargeable
1	92.5	1	0
2	85.0	2	0
3	77.5	3	95
4	70.0	4	90
5	62.5	5	85
6	55.0	6	80
7	47.5	7	75
8	40.0	8	70
9	32.5	9	65
10 or more	25.0	10 or more	60

Transfers of assets between spouses do not give rise to any gain or loss with the acquiring spouse standing in the shoes of the disposing spouse. Where assets are to be sold at a substantial gain it is worth considering transferring ownership before the disposal takes place. Two advantages can be gained from this step. The first is that as both husband and wife have an annual exemption it is possible to make use of both by careful planning. The second is that the rate of tax applied to the taxable gain is worked out by treating the gain as though it was the top slice of income. If one spouse is liable at the higher rate of 40 per cent, for example, and the other at a lower rate of 23 per cent, the asset could be transferred to the spouse with the lower tax rate. It should be noted that the level of gains does not count as income for the purpose of entitlement to age allowances. 3.81

TABLE 3.5

Estimating expenditure	Weekly expenditure	Monthly expenditure	Annual expenditure
Food and drink			
Clothing			
Mortgate interest			
Electricity/Gas/Oil			
Telephone			
Maintenance and repairs			
Insurances			
Subscriptions			
Deeds of covenant			
Car running costs			
• Petrol • Service and repairs • Breakdown service • Insurance • Road tax • Depreciation			
Social and entertainment expenditure			
Holidays			
Healthcare insurance premiums			
Birthdays/Christmas gifts			
Other			
	———	———	———
	× 52 =		
		× 12 =	
	Total spendable income requirement		
	Taxation		
	Gross income requirement		

Chapter 4

DISPOSING OF A BUSINESS

Many people spend their working life building up successful businesses. In the approach to retirement an important issue which may have to be addressed is what will happen to their interest in the business on retirement. **4.1**

The form of the business can vary. The business may be carried on in incorporated form in which case the asset owned will be shares in the company. Income may have been drawn from such a company in the form of salary, by way of dividend, or both. An unincorporated business may have been carried on by a sole trader or in partnership with others. In that case the taxable income from the business will have been equal to its profits while drawings will have determined the spendable income of the proprietor. **4.2**

Those who have their own business should consider as early as possible providing for pension. The more pension provision can be separated from the value of the business itself by making independent provision, the easier it will be to retire at a time of the individual's own choosing. Unfortunately, the demands of a growing business can often outweigh pension planning and the capital tied up in the business becomes the main source of income in retirement. If that is the case the capital has to be released or has to generate income into the future when retirement occurs. That means some decisions will have to be made as to the future of the business. There are a number of alternatives. **4.3**

A company shareholder may: **4.4**
- Retain the shares and appoint a manager to run the business. Dividend income may continue to be

received, but for businesses which were previously owner-managed, the profits which support this will be lower by the amount of any salary paid to the manager.
- Sell the shares to a third party.
- Sell or gift the shares to a member of the family. This may be particularly relevant if the company is going to stay in family ownership and be run by future generations.
- Wind the company up, selling off its assets, paying its liabilities and liquidating it.
- If there is another shareholder, the company may purchase its own shares.

4.5 *The self-employed may:*
- Employ a manager to run the business.
- Withdraw from a partnership, receiving accumulated capital in the business. This may include a payment for goodwill.
- Bring in a member of the family as a partner to run the business in future.
- Sell the business as a going concern to a third party.
- Sell the business assets and pay off its liabilities, thus winding it up.

4.6 The strategy chosen will depend on the structure of the business, whether there is succession as to management, the extent to which it is dependent on the personal skills of the owner, and the need for capital to be released from the business in retirement.

4.7 For those who have a choice there may be tax issues which affect the decision. These fall into three broad categories:
- income tax
- capital gains tax
- inheritance tax.

Income tax issues

4.8 Discontinuing a business carried on by a sole trader will involve realising its assets including the closing stock and work in progress of that business. Where that stock is sold either to a customer or to someone who will carry on the business, generally the price paid for the stock is that agreed between these third parties. In some cases, such as the transfer of the business to a connected person (for example, a son or daughter), the value that must be accounted for is market value. That disposal value will have a direct effect on quantifying the amount of the taxable profit for the final accounting period of the business.

4.9 Other assets such as debtors may also have an effect. Provided accounts have been prepared on a full earnings basis annually (*i.e.* including stock and debtors), it is likely that all profits will thus be brought into tax for the tax year of cessation. Profits which arise after cessation and that have not been taxed (perhaps because the business has been assessed on a cash basis), are taxed as received under Schedule D, Case 6.

4.10 When a business is sold, the assets may be sold for a lump sum or the sale agreement may stipulate that the proceeds should be allocated to specific assets. The allocation must be reasonable but within that, in the case of third party sales, the Inland Revenue will normally be bound by the allocation of price as agreed between the parties. This can result in tax savings being made—for example, if the business has losses brought forward, if there is scope to allocate more to stock the final profits may be increased, enabling them to be offset against the losses.

4.11 The general rule that applies to an ongoing business is that profits earned for an accounting period of 12 months ending in a tax year are taxed in that year. For example, profits for the year ended June 30, 1998 are taxed in 1998/99. In the tax year in which a business is permanently discontinued, the taxable profits will usually be those from the end of the last basis period until the date of cessation. If, for example, the above business ceased on January 31, 1999, its basis period for 1998/99 would be from July 1, 1997 to January 31, 1999. This is a much simpler system than the one which applied prior to 1997/98 when some profits could drop out of assessment altogether and others could be assessed twice.

4.12 There are some vestiges left over from that old system, and if a business ceases before April 6, 1999, it may result in a revision to the profits assessed for 1996/97 to that arising between April 6, 1996 and April 5, 1997. (Cessations before April 6, 1998 may result in the old system applying right up to the end of the business.)

4.13 A special relief called overlap relief is available in the year of cessation. This relief allows the taxable profits for the final year to be reduced by the amount of any overlap profits. Overlap profits normally arise when a business first commences or on a change of accounting date. A special transitional overlap profit arises for those whose business had commenced before April 6, 1994 and continued after April 6, 1997. That transitional overlap profit is the amount of profit arising after the end of the basis period for 1996/97 (usually the 12-month accounting period ending in that tax year) and before April 6, 1997. By way of example, a businessman with an accounting period ending on June 30, 1996 would have an overlap profit based on his profits for the period July 1, 1996 to April 5, 1997. It can be many years between overlap profits arising and a tax deduction for them becoming available and as a result it is vital that a careful record is kept of any relief due.

4.14 In addition to the above points the sale of assets such as plant and machinery on which capital allowances have been claimed can give rise to a balancing charge or allowance which further affects taxable profits. Again this should be considered carefully in allocating proceeds on sale against specific assets, but as such an allocation may also affect the amount on which a buyer can claim capital allowances, there may be an element of negotiation required.

4.15 Partners in partnerships have similar issues on retirement. Provided at least one partner continues in business both before and after the retirement the partnership business itself automatically continues, notwithstanding that legally the partnership may dissolve. Each partner's share of profits is allocated individually and the cessation rules apply to that share if the partner ceases to carry on the business. The retiring partner may be assessed on a different allocation of profits than his fellow partners. For example, if a firm draws up accounts to June 30, 1998 and a partner retires on December 31, 1998, the ongoing partners would be assessed in 1998/99 on their share of profits for the year ended June 30, 1998. The retiring partner would be assessed in 1998/99 on his share of profits for the period July 1, 1997 to December 31, 1998 less any overlap relief to which he was personally entitled.

A sole trader might consider bringing in a partner to his business prior to winding it up as a means of avoiding the cessation of the business as well as smoothing any transition to new management. **4.16**

In this section it is only possible to give a flavour of the income tax issues which have to be addressed on retirement and disposal of a business by whatever means. There is no substitute for reviewing the position closely in the years running up to retirement with a view to identifying the specific issues and the options available. The timing of retirement or sale of a business can be critical in determining the taxable profits and careful planning can result in significant reductions of the income tax bill due. **4.17**

Capital gains tax issues

Selling a business or shares in a company is likely to involve the disposal of chargeable assets for capital gains tax purposes. Sometimes these are not tangible assets but may include items such as goodwill. The gains on such assets may well substantially exceed any annual exemption available and if the proceeds are destined to fund retirement it can make a significant difference if the proceeds are subject to a tax charge at 40 per cent. It is therefore well worth exploring planning options which will reduce such a tax burden and, again, allocation of the sale proceeds can help in this area. **4.18**

Retirement relief

A major relief from capital gains tax which should be explored is retirement relief. This relief is available to **4.19**

84   *Money Matters*

individuals who have attained the age of 50, or who have retired on ill-health grounds, and who dispose of business assets and meet the conditions for the relief, described below. Note that retirement is not a requirement for relief to apply—it is enough that the requisite age has been reached if the other conditions are met. The relief is available on disposals in years of assessment up to 2002/03. Thereafter the relief is withdrawn.

4.20 The maximum amount of relief depends on two factors—the size of the gain and the length of time the qualifying conditions have been met. Gains in column 2 of Table 4.1 are fully exempt. Gains in excess of the figure in column 2 up to the limit in column 3 are taxed as though 50 per cent were exempt. Gains in excess of the figure in column 3 are taxed in full.

TABLE 4.1: Retirement relief

Tax year of disposal	Fully exempt limit	50% exempt limit
1998/99	£250,000	£1,000,000
1999/00	£200,000	£800,000
2000/01	£150,000	£600,000
2001/02	£100,000	£400,000
2002/03	£50,000	£200,000

4.21 The exemption limits in Table 4.1 apply where the requisite conditions have been satisfied throughout a 10-year period ending with the date of disposal. If the period in which they have been satisfied ending on that date is less than 10 years, the amount of the exemption in each column is scaled down. The scale rises arithmetically from 10 per cent where the period is exactly one year to 100 per cent where the conditions have been satisfied for 10 years. For example, if a gain is realised of £400,000 in 1998/99 and the conditions have been satisfied for three years exactly, £75,000 (30 per cent of £250,000) would be exempt and £112,500, being 50 per cent of £225,000 (30 per cent of £1,000,000 less £250,000), would also be exempt. The remaining £100,000 would be taxed in full.

The conditions that apply vary according to whether the gain **4.22**
arises on:

(1) the disposal of the business or part of a business;
(2) the disposal of assets in use for the purposes of the business at the time it ceases to be carried on;
(3) the disposal of shares or securities in a company;
(4) the disposal of an asset held for the purposes of an employment;
(5) the disposal of business assets owned by an individual and used by a partnership or company; and
(6) in certain circumstances the disposal of assets held by a trust.

In the case of a disposal of a business, a distinction must be **4.23**
made between the disposal of some of the assets of a business and the disposal of a part of the business itself. This distinction is often a fine one and there have been a series of cases before the courts in which this has been examined. These cases have predominantly concerned the farming industry. The leading case is *McGregor v. Adcock*[1] where a farmer disposed of a field on his farm and claimed relief on the basis that he had disposed of part of his business. This was rejected. This case and the subsequent cases[2] have established a test known as the "interference test" to decide whether a disposal is significant enough to represent a disposal of a part of a business. The business activities before and after the sale should be compared. If the activities which make up the business after the sale are wholly different from those carried on before, the disposal can be regarded as a sale of part of the business. This test can be difficult to apply in practice since it first means analysing all the myriad activities that can be involved in a business and then deciding if these activities have changed to a significant degree. The lesson which must be observed is that disposing of a business piecemeal can be dangerous and can result in the loss of retirement relief. It is better to ensure that the assets are disposed of at the same time.

---

[1] [1977] S.T.C. 206.
[2] *Mannion v. Johnston* [1988] S.T.C. 578; *Atkinson v. Dancer* [1988] S.T.C. 758; *Pepper v. Daffurn* [1993] S.T.C. 466; *Jarmin v. Rawlings* [1994] S.T.C. 1005; and *Wase v. Bourke* [1996] S.T.C. 18.

4.24 Subject to this fundamental point the main requirement to qualify for relief is that the business is owned for a period of at least one year ending with the disposal. The relief is extended to assets which were in use for the purposes of a business owned by the individual for at least one year at the time that business ceased. The disposal must take place within one year of the business ceasing. An example might be property which was leased rent-free by the individual to his business and was disposed of at the same time as the business ceased or within a year of its cessation. The Inland Revenue can permit a longer period in special circumstances but this extension is very rare.

4.25 Where the disposal is of shares or securities in a company the conditions that require to be met for a minimum period of a year are:

(1) The company must be a trading company or the holding company of a trading group.
(2) The individual must be able to exercise not less than 5 per cent of the voting rights in the company. This makes it a "personal" company.
(3) The individual must be a full-time working director of the company or a member of its group. A full-time working director is not defined but Revenue practice is to consider the company's normal working week. Provided the individual works at least three-quarters of these hours he will be regarded as a full-time working director. If the individual has ceased to be a full-time working director but devotes at least 10 hours per week on average to the service of the company in a technical or managerial capacity to the date of disposal he will still qualify for relief. Should the retirement be occasioned by a period of illness which prevents the individual from working, the Inland Revenue treat him as continuing in full-time employment for about a year provided there is no evidence that he will be unable to return to work in that period.

4.26 Care needs to be taken that the whole of the gain arising on the shares qualifies for relief. If the balance sheet of the company contains non-business assets there may be a restriction. The restriction is the proportion that the chargeable business assets of the company bear to its total chargeable assets. A chargeable asset is one on which a taxable gain would arise if it was sold for proceeds worth more than its cost. Non-chargeable assets such as cash are ignored. A similar test is applied to assets of groups of companies where the shareholding disposed of is in the holding company.

Trust holdings

If the company is the individual's "personal" company, as defined above, and he is a full-time working director, any shares owned by a trust of which he is a beneficiary entitled to its income as of right will also qualify for relief. **4.27**

Where trustees dispose of an asset used in a business carried on by the individual, and he has an entitlement to the income of the trust, relief will be available if the asset is a chargeable business asset and the asset has been used in the individual's business throughout a period of at least one year ending with the date of disposal. The individual must have ceased to carry on the business on the date of disposal, or within the period of 12 months before. **4.28**

If there are non-qualifying beneficiaries of the trust as well as the qualifying beneficiary, then the gain is split with only the proportion attributable to the qualifying beneficiary obtaining relief. **4.29**

Ill health

If retirement takes place on grounds of ill health, the Inland Revenue may launch an enquiry into the individual's tax return in which the relief has been deducted. If they do so, evidence that he is incapable of engaging in work of the kind he previously undertook and is likely to remain permanently so incapable, may be called for. The Revenue employ their own Medical Officer to examine this evidence and a medical examination may be required. **4.30**

4.31 A claim to retirement relief is not required and the relief is given automatically when the conditions are met. Special provisions apply to make relief available if successive businesses are carried on within the 10-year period.

Withdrawal of retirement relief

4.32 Although retirement relief is being phased out it is replaced by taper relief which increases according to the length of time the asset is held. As taper relief is not a complete exemption, while retirement relief is in part, there are winners and losers to this change in the tax legislation. Those with smaller gains which would have benefited from complete exemption are likely to be worse off compared to those with high gains who would have been taxed in full on the excess of gains over £1,000,000. Those in between may gain or lose. Figure 4.1 illustrates the position:

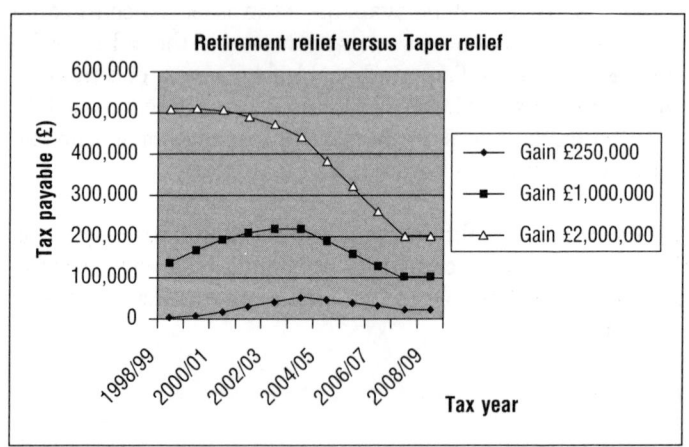

Fig. 4.1

4.33 For those in the "loser" category but who are in the approach to retirement and already meet the qualifying conditions, it is worth considering whether the gain can be crystallised early to enable the benefit of retirement relief to be obtained. In considering this option bear in mind that actual retirement is not necessary.

Disposing of a Business

A further planning point is to watch shares or securities held by a non-qualifying spouse. If the other spouse already qualifies for relief and all the shares are to be sold, it may pay to transfer the shares between the spouses (the transfer being tax free) so that relief is obtained. **4.34**

Apart from retirement relief, other capital gains tax reliefs may be worthy of consideration. Specific reliefs that may apply are: **4.35**

- Rollover relief
- Enterprise Investment Scheme relief
- Venture Capital Trust relief.

As these reliefs involve either reinvesting in new business assets or new companies they are less likely to be suitable for the elderly reaching retirement age and are not considered further in this book. It is worth noting that the latter two are high-risk investments but, for those faced with a significant tax bill on disposal of a business, they may be worthy of examination in appropriate circumstances.

Purchase of own shares

As an alternative to selling shares to third parties, where there is another shareholder in a company the company can buy back its own shares. Such a purchase of own shares may be taxed in one of two ways. Generally it will be taxed as a distribution which means that it will be liable to income tax in the hands of the recipient and the company will be liable to account for advance corporation tax on the proceeds (until April 6, 1999). If certain conditions are met it may be taxed as a capital receipt liable to capital gains tax. The first condition is that the purchase must not have as its motive the avoidance of tax and must benefit the company's trade. If it is entered into to facilitate the retiral of a controlling shareholder as a director, the Revenue accept that this benefits the company's trade. (Another justification for capital treatment is that the proceeds are applied in meeting inheritance tax on the death of the shareholder.) The shareholder must have owned the shares for a period of at least five years. Other conditions require the shareholder to reduce his interest by a **4.36** substantial amount, to be resident in the United Kingdom and not to be connected with the company after the sale.

Extracting cash before sale

4.37 Other matters which should be considered before selling shares in a company are whether there is benefit in paying a dividend before sale. Such a dividend will be liable to higher rates of income tax if appropriate less the tax credit for advance corporation tax payable by the company. If the company can offset the advance corporation tax against its corporation tax liability such a pre-sale dividend, which will lower the price to be paid for the shares, may be more tax effective than subjecting the proceeds for the shares to capital gains tax.

4.38 Another option may be for the company to top up a pension scheme and enhance benefits payable. Again this reduces the value of the company by the amount paid, but may be more effective in giving value to the shareholder/employee. The scope of this route is subject to Inland Revenue limits.

4.39 A common belief is that a retiring director can receive an *ex gratia* payment from the company of up to £30,000 tax free. However, a terminal payment made on or in anticipation of retirement is not exempt and the Inland Revenue would be certain to challenge such an arrangement on retirement.

Succession

4.40 When a business features in retirement planning, the key is to plan ahead. A business can rarely be sold quickly and time should be taken to examine all options. If the business is to be retained but managed and run by someone else, consider carefully if they have the skills to do so. Unless they have a proprietorial interest they may not be as dedicated to the business as the outgoing owner. Ways may have to be found to provide an incentive. Consideration needs to be given to whether the business can afford a manager or whether it would be better just to sell up.

Similarly, if a partner is to be introduced, there needs to be **4.41**
time given for any handover and to ensure clients or customers can be transferred smoothly to the new contact. Consideration needs to be given to whether the new partner should compensate the outgoing partner for goodwill and how much capital he should contribute to the business, bearing in mind the capital to be withdrawn by the outgoing partner.

If shares in a company are to be retained, it may be the case **4.42**
that salary income will be replaced by dividend income. Again the company will have to replace the contribution made by the outgoing owner by employing someone to do his work. While the reward for this may not be as much as that required to compensate someone with capital invested in the company, it may still limit the ability to distribute the same level of income as was expected before. Dividend income can only be paid if the company has reserves out of which it can make distributions and this too may be a limiting factor. All shareholders have to be treated equally, so if the shares are not 100 per cent owned this may be an issue. Possibilities of addressing this include reorganising capital and perhaps using preference shares.

Inheritance tax issues

As will be seen in Chapter 5, most businesses qualify for **4.43**
relief from inheritance tax of up to 100 per cent. One consequence of selling a business is that this relief will be lost. Overnight the shareholder could find that his exposure to this tax has increased dramatically and it is sensible to review the exposure to this tax and consider what planning steps could be taken to mitigate it. Generally this review should be undertaken before the sale takes place as it may be easier and more tax effective to pass wealth from the business on to family before a sale rather than after.

This chapter summarises some of the considerations that **4.44**
have to be taken into account in disposing of a business on retirement. Finding a buyer of the business can be difficult. There may be an obvious purchaser or the business could be

advertised in trade journals. In other cases the help of a corporate financier such as a firm of chartered accountants or a merchant bank may be appropriate. As individual circumstances vary considerably, it will pay to take professional advice well before the sale takes place both in terms of maximising the opportunities available and in mitigating tax on disposal.

CHAPTER 5

ESTATE PLANNING

When a person dies, their assets pass to their heirs either under a will or by operation of law. This is considered in more depth in Chapter 7. The amount that is inherited is subject to taxes charged on death. Most people would prefer their estate to pass to their heirs rather than into the public coffers, and this chapter examines some planning steps that can be taken to minimise tax on death. **5.1**

The tax that applies on death is called inheritance tax. This tax is badly named—it applies not to the sum inherited but to the value of the estate held on death calculated at the moment before death. The deceased is treated as making a transfer of all of his or her property at that time. Furthermore, it applies not just on death but also to certain transfers of assets during lifetime. **5.2**

Certain property is treated as if it is within a person's estate for the purposes of computing the tax charge. The most common example is a trust which gives the right to a person to receive the income from the trust fund during their lifetime (liferent trusts). Where a person has such a right, the assets of the whole fund may be treated as if that person owns them. On the liferenter's death the value of the assets in the trust at that time is aggregated with the rest of their estate for the purpose of computing inheritance tax liabilities. **5.3**

To establish the rate of tax at death, all lifetime transfers within the previous seven years are cumulated and are added to the value of the estate at date of death. Currently, once the cumulative value exceeds £223,000 a flat rate of tax **5.4** at 40 per cent applies to the value of property in excess of this figure.

5.5 Lifetime gifts are taxed much more favourably than assets held on death. The value of the gift is measured by the loss to the donor's estate. To the extent that the gift is made to an individual or into most types of trust it is exempt, unless the donor dies within seven years of making the gift. Such a gift is called a potentially exempt transfer, commonly abbreviated to a PET. Where the donor does die within seven years of making the gift, it is taxed as the first tranche of the estate at the tax rates that apply at time of death. If tax is payable it is abated by a taper relief if death occurs more than three years after the gift. The taper relief applies to abate the rate of tax payable to the following amounts:

- transfer more than 3 years and not more than 4 years before the death—80 per cent
- transfer more than 4 years and not more than 5 years before the death—60 per cent
- transfer more than 5 years and not more than 6 years before the death—40 per cent
- transfer more than 6 years and not more than 7 years before the death—20 per cent.

5.6 Tax on lifetime gifts is rarely payable at the time of the gift as a result of these rules, and the main occasion of charge is a gift into a discretionary settlement (that is a trust where the beneficiary is not entitled to the income as of right). Where a charge arises the value transferred is not just the amount of the gift but also the tax payable (unless the donee pays it) and thus the gift has to be grossed up.

5.7 The tax rates applicable for inheritance tax are currently:

- First £223,000 of cumulative chargeable lifetime transfers and assets on death—Nil.
- Cumulative lifetime transfers in excess of £223,000 made more than seven years prior to death, where chargeable—20%.
- Estate on death and lifetime transfers within seven years of death above £223,000—40%.

Estate Planning

5.8 It can readily be seen that one way of avoiding inheritance tax is to give away assets during lifetime. There are three practical considerations that must be reviewed in adopting such a strategy. First, can the person afford to give away assets? Secondly, will a capital gains tax liability arise on the gift? Thirdly, can the gift be made without a reservation of benefit? These three questions are now examined more fully.

Giving away assets

5.9 The effect on income and on security is paramount—after all, inheritance tax is really the heirs' problem not the individual's! No one should be encouraged to impoverish himself or herself just to save tax. Many people take the confident view that should they need the funds, the family to whom they have gifted them will take care of them. That view may well be right, but nobody can foresee the future. What happens if the family member predeceases the donor? Could the assets pass to their spouse who might remarry? What if the donee spends the assets or becomes bankrupt? What might happen if the donee divorces? However unlikely these issues may appear at the time of the gift, they can arise and hence pose a threat to family security.

Capital gains tax

5.10 Capital gains tax is another issue. Apart from cash, most assets will give rise to a potential capital gains tax liability if gifted. The tax payable on the gain might be as high as 40 per cent, the same as the death rate of inheritance tax. While it is the gain that is taxed and not the whole value of the asset, if that gain is a high proportion of the asset there is no point in realising a tax liability earlier than would be the case on death. Many people are unaware that on death, assets are revalued at market value at date of death but are not subject to capital gains tax. There is a tax-free uplift on death. In making lifetime gifts it is usually desirable to structure the gift so that no capital gains tax is payable. An important relief from capital gains tax in this connection is holdover relief.

Holdover relief

5.11 Holdover relief is a deferral of capital gains tax which is available when certain assets are gifted or transferred under a bargain other than one at arm's length. When this relief is claimed, the donor's capital gain is reduced to nil but the acquisition value of the donee, which is usually the open market value of the asset, is reduced by a corresponding amount. This means that when the donee in turn disposes of the asset, the gain he or she makes is increased by the donor's gain.

5.12 *Example*:

An asset is acquired for £10,000. When gifted its market value is £30,000 and there is indexation of £8,000 available.

The donor would normally have a gain of £12,000. This is reduced to nil. The donee would normally acquire the asset at a value of £30,000. This is reduced to £18,000.

If the donee then sells the asset for £40,000 there is a gain of £22,000, being £10,000 since acquisition of the asset and the deferred gain of £12,000.

5.13 Not all gains on gifts are eligible for the relief. Gains on business assets are available for relief, in the case of individuals, if they are:

- assets used for the purposes of a trade or profession carried on by the transferor;
- assets used for the purpose of a trade or profession carried on by a company in which the transferor has 5 per cent of the voting rights. This also extends to assets so used by members of a trading group in which the transferor has 5 per cent of the voting rights in the holding company;
- shares or securities in a trading company or group which are not listed;
- shares or securities of a trading company or group which are listed but in which the transferor owns 5 per cent of the voting rights;
- assets which are agricultural property for inheritance tax purposes and would qualify for agricultural property relief.

Estate Planning

5.14 There are restrictions to the relief where the asset was not used for trading purposes throughout its period of ownership or, in the case of shares and securities, where the company's assets are not all chargeable business assets.

5.15 Individuals qualify for relief whether the gift is made to another individual, a trust or a company. Trustees also qualify for relief on transfers to individuals or other trusts. The donee must be resident and ordinarily resident in the United Kingdom for tax purposes before relief is granted. The relief must be claimed and both donor and donee must sign the claim for relief, except in the case of a gift to a trust, where only the donor need claim.

5.16 Transfers which are chargeable transfers for inheritance tax also qualify for relief. The most common example is a gift to a discretionary trust. Transfers which are potentially exempt transfers are excluded, so gifts to individuals do not fall into this category. Relief does extend to certain transfers, which have specific exemptions from inheritance tax so no tax is actually payable. Chargeable transfers within the nil rate band of inheritance tax, for example, qualify for relief.

5.17 There is a danger in claiming holdover relief. If the donee becomes not resident and not ordinarily resident within six years of the end of the tax year in which the gift is made, the heldover gain crystallises at that time. The capital gains tax is payable by the donee, but if, having left the country, he fails to pay within 12 months of its due date, the Inland Revenue can recover the tax from the donor. The donor then has a right of recovery from the donee, although there may be practical difficulties in exercising this under foreign jurisdictions.

5.18 Assets held in trust are deemed to have been disposed of when someone entitled to the trust income dies. Normally in such a case the trust assets are revalued at market value but no capital gain arises. However, where the trust assets include assets on which there are heldover gains, the heldover gain crystallises and tax becomes payable.

Reservation of benefit

5.19 Reserving a benefit in the asset gifted must also be avoided. If such a benefit is reserved then the asset is treated as remaining in the donor's estate and the gift is ineffective in reducing the value of the estate. Indeed, when the reservation is released, this can be another occasion of charge and while there are complex rules to avoid double taxation, a gift with reservation is best avoided altogether. What constitutes a gift with reservation? In simple terms, if the donor or spouse continue to have any sort of benefit or enjoyment of the asset, now or in the future, there will be a reservation of benefit. A simple example would be if the donor gifted paintings to his children but left them hanging on the walls of his house. Death benefits from pension schemes are not regarded as giving rise to a reservation of benefit.

5.20 Many elderly people look to their house as a possible asset they could give away during lifetime to their children. As the house generates no income they hope that they can reduce the value of their estate for inheritance tax purposes without affecting their standard of living. Unfortunately this is a very high-risk strategy because of the gift with reservation rules. If the donor intends to continue living in the house he will only be able to do so if he pays a full arm's length rental for it. If the rental is undervalued by even one pound, there will be a reservation of benefit in all of it. One way around this, often suggested as a solution, is to carve out an interest in the property before it is gifted, and then to gift only the part subject to the interest taken. This might be achieved by taking a lease of the property at a peppercorn rent and then gifting the landlord's interest subject to the lease. In Scots law it is not possible to grant a lease to yourself and so achieving a carve-out of a tenant's interest before the gift is extremely difficult. The scheme is made more difficult by the fact that a lease of property cannot exceed 20 years. This needs to be compared with life expectancy of the donor.

5.21 The Revenue accept that if a house is put into joint ownership with the donor and donee each owning a part, the part gifted will not be a gift with reservation if the donee lives in it provided all outgoings over the property are shared proportionately to the ownership.

Lifetime gifts

Aside from problems with reservations of benefit outright lifetime gifts benefit from several exemptions which take the assets outwith the charge to inheritance tax even if death occurs within seven years. The main exemption is the annual exemption. This exempts the first £3,000 of outright gifts made in any tax year. To the extent that this exemption is not used in any year, it can be carried forward for one year only. 5.22

Example: 5.23
The donor makes a gift of £4,000 in 1998/99. No previous gifts have been made. The exemption available is the 1998/99 exemption of £3,000 and £1,000 carried forward from 1997/98. No part of the annual exemption is available to carry forward to 1999/2000.

A second useful exemption is the small gift exemption. This exempts gifts of up to £250 per person per tax year. There is no limit to the number of gifts that can be made, but if the limit of £250 is exceeded to any one person the exemption is lost. The prime purpose of the exemption is to exclude birthday and Christmas presents and other small gifts from charge to tax. This exemption is applied before the annual exemption. 5.24

Another important exemption is that for gifts which are normal expenditure out of income. This exemption is often assumed to apply in circumstances where it does not and the conditions for it to apply need to be carefully considered. There are three legs to the exemption: 5.25

    (a) the gift must be made as part of the normal expenditure of the transferor, and
    (b) (taking one year with another) it must be made out of his income, and
    (c) after allowing for all transfers of value forming part of his normal expenditure, the transferor must be left with sufficient income to maintain his usual standard of living.

5.26 "Normal" is considered to mean in this context "typical" or "habitual". The meaning of normal was considered in the case of *Bennett v. IRC*.[1] While there is no fixed minimum period during which the expenditure must have occurred, it is necessary that the pattern of actual or intended regular payments is established and the expenditure in question conforms with that pattern.

5.27 An individual's income is calculated on normal principles and is not necessarily the same as his income for tax purposes. The capital element of an annuity will be excluded from income, as will 5 per cent withdrawals from life insurance bonds. Fluctuations of income from one year to another can be averaged out.

5.28 The onus is on the taxpayer to show that all three conditions are satisfied and hence if a claim for relief is made, sufficient evidence must be available to support the claim. Once a pattern of expenditure is established relief should be available even if the pattern does not last for long. For example, if the donor makes one payment under an annual life assurance policy, then dies, relief should be available provided there is evidence he intended to continue paying premiums on behalf of the donee annually.

5.29 There are a number of other exemptions from inheritance tax available that may also be applicable and brief details are given below.

- Gifts of between £1,000 and £5,000 in anticipation of marriage. The exact amount depends on the relationship of the donor to the donee. Each parent of either party to the marriage can make an exempt gift of £5,000 and each grandparent can make a gift of £2,500.
- Payments for family maintenance (*i.e.* spouse and minor children).
- Gifts to certain favoured bodies (*e.g.* registered charities).
- Gifts of certain favoured types of property (*e.g.* heritage property).

---

[1] [1995] S.T.C. 54.

Spouse exemption

One very important exemption from inheritance tax is the spouse exemption. Any assets passing between husband and wife, whether during lifetime or on death, are exempt. The only exception is where the spouses have different domiciles. In that case the exemption is limited to £55,000. This exemption can be used very effectively in planning for inheritance tax. Perhaps most importantly it means that on the first of husband and wife to die, the survivor's resources are not reduced by the payment of tax.

5.30

Secondly, as both husband and wife each have a band of assets worth £223,000 which are taxed at a nil rate, by careful division of the combined estate between them, up to £446,000 can be left to the heirs without payment of tax. In order to make use of the nil rate band each spouse must own at least the amount of the nil rate at date of death. This involves equalising estates to at least this extent by lifetime gifting. This exercise should not be carried out in isolation of its other consequences.

5.31

It has been shown in Chapter 1 that by ensuring each spouse has income, lower rates of income tax can be paid by using personal allowances and lower rate bands. Similarly, if each spouse makes disposals for capital gains tax each benefits from the annual capital gains tax exemption. Typically one spouse might have high pension income and hence the other might hold all the investments to generate investment income. It can be seen that ownership of assets for income tax purposes might fly in direct contradiction to the best split of ownership for inheritance tax and capital gains tax, and a balance must be struck.

5.32

The most valuable asset a couple own is often their home. This can be used to equalise ownership but care must be taken over how title to the property is held. In Scotland property owned jointly is often held under a "special destination". Typically this provides that property is held jointly and on the death of the first spouse it passes to the second automatically regardless of the terms of a will. If

5.33

advantage of the nil rate band is to be obtained twice, the property held at date of death must be capable of passing to someone other than the spouse.

5.34 The question of whether a house should pass to children on the first death is not without risk. Under Scots law, a joint owner of property who wishes to sell his share when the other joint owner does not, can enforce a sale by an action of division and sale. This creates a risk for the surviving spouse who may want to stay on in the home when the children oppose this. On the other hand a child can own the half share inherited on death, without any risk of the reservation of benefit legislation applying to the surviving spouse.

5.35 Use of a half share of the house to utilise the nil rate band has the advantage that it may not affect income-producing resources which the surviving spouse needs to live on. For that reason it remains the prime focus of most married couples in estate planning.

5.36 For those who have the resources, planning to give the nil rate band to the children on the death of the first spouse can result in tax savings of over £89,000 measured over both deaths. However, Scots law does not give complete freedom over how the estate can be divided. The law of succession provides for a division of the estate between spouse and children regardless of whether a will is drawn up or the individual dies intestate. Those entitled to legal rights in an estate, which are described more fully in Chapter 7, can disclaim their entitlement.

Will planning

5.37 Although leaving assets direct to heirs other than the spouse to the value of the nil rate band can significantly reduce the tax charge on assets ultimately passing to the family, an issue often encountered is concern that by doing this the surviving spouse will have insufficient assets to live on. Similar concerns can arise if there are elderly parents or other dependants who might need support. A way around this is to leave assets equivalent to the nil rate band to a discretionary trust

Estate Planning

in which the spouse, dependants and other family are all potential beneficiaries. As the value of lifetime gifts, such as failed PETs, which will be cumulated with the estate on death will not necessarily be known, and the value of the nil rate band increases, usually annually, it is a good idea to word the legacy to the discretionary trust in such a way that the amount varies to use up the remaining part of the nil rate band. An example of a legacy which varies in this way is shown by the following wording:

> "I leave such sum ('the nil rate band legacy') as is equal to the upper limit of the nil per cent rate band (applicable on my death) in the table of rates of tax in Schedule 1 to the Inheritance Tax Act 1984 less an amount equal to the aggregate of the amount chargeable to inheritance tax of:
>
> (i) all or any chargeable transfers (including potentially exempt transfers which have become chargeable as a result of my death) made by me during my lifetime in the cumulation period specified by section 7(1)(a) of the Inheritance Tax Act 1984, and
>
> (ii) all other gifts (if any) taking effect under my Will or any codicil to my Will to the extent that they are not exempt transfers for the purposes of the charge to inheritance tax on my death, and
>
> (iii) all other property (if any) which is treated as property to which I am beneficially entitled immediately before my death (including property subject to a reservation as defined by section 102 of the Finance Act 1986), and
>
> (iv) all or any settled property in which on my death I have an interest in possession (as that expression has meaning for the purposes of the Inheritance Tax Act 1984) and which is chargeable to inheritance tax by reason of my death,
>
> to ....".

5.38 By using a discretionary trust, the trustees have the power to apply income and capital for any beneficiary according to their view of that beneficiary's needs. However, the capital in the trust does not form part of that beneficiary's estate on death. The trust itself is liable to inheritance tax charges every 10 years and when capital leaves the trust. The rate of tax applicable to a discretionary trust is calculated in a complex manner but where the trust is established using the nil rate band, the effective tax rate for the first 10 years of the trust is zero per cent. Thereafter the tax rate may increase according to the value of assets in it but under current rules and tax rates can never exceed 6 per cent and is often much lower. As a result the assets plus their growth in value can be kept out of the surviving spouse's estate while the use of the capital is still possible. Obviously this puts a lot of responsibility in the hands of the trustees, who should therefore be carefully selected, and the wishes of the settlor as to the use of the funds should be clearly spelled out before entering into this type of arrangement.

Death benefits under pension schemes

5.39 Most occupational pension schemes offer a death in service benefit should the employee die before drawing pension. The maximum permissible benefit is four times the salary payable and this is usually payable at the discretion of the pension scheme trustees. Although this gives the trustees complete discretion over whom they pay the benefit to, they are often guided by the wishes of the employee. In the absence of any expressed wishes they will usually pay it to his estate or to his spouse. It may be advantageous to make a death in service benefit the subject of an expression of wish that the trustees pay it to named beneficiaries. The benefits are not liable to inheritance tax unless either the executors have a legally enforceable claim to the benefits (which is not the case if they are payable at the discretion of the pension scheme trustees) or the deceased had the power (as distinct from making an unenforceable suggestion) to nominate or appoint the benefits to any person. Any part of the lump sum nominated to the spouse would form part of the spouse's estate on subsequent death. The lump sum can be an extremely effective way to fund any inheritance tax payable on the estate and for this reason it is not always advisable to nominate the spouse as the recipient. Subject to considering family requirements, as a principle the death benefit should be directed to those beneficiaries who will ultimately inherit the estate and bear the tax on it. It would be possible to nominate that the benefits from the policy be paid to a discretionary trust of which the spouse and other members of the family were all beneficiaries.

In the case of retirement annuities or personal pensions the death in service benefit can consist of a refund of premiums paid, with or without interest, or in the case of unitised policies, a return of the value of the fund. This death benefit can be written in trust for the benefit of dependants so that it does not form part of the estate of the deceased policyholder. As the policyholder can choose the age at which he draws pension up to age 75, it could be argued that he has failed to exercise a right as a result of which the value of his estate has diminished, if he defers drawing pension. This would be an occasion of charge to inheritance tax. The Inland Revenue do not take this point where the motive of paying pension premiums is genuinely to provide retirement benefits. If the motive in not taking up benefits is to benefit someone else, the Revenue will consider raising a claim to tax. In particular this applies if the policyholder is in poor health to the extent that life assurance was not available or was suffering from a terminal illness if either a new policy was taken out after that time or the death benefits under existing policies were assigned. It also applies if further single premiums or enhanced annual premiums are paid to existing policies or the date for deferring retirement is deferred after that time. Although rare, this limits "deathbed" planning with pensions and it is advisable to consider carefully how the benefits should be written at the outset. **5.40**

Funding inheritance tax through life assurance

If death occurs after retirement when pension is drawn, the death benefit from a pension scheme will not be available to fund inheritance tax. Beneficiaries of the estate will therefore have to consider selling assets to raise sufficient funds to meet any inheritance tax liability. This liability commonly **5.41** arises on the second to die of husband and wife. As the point of death may not always be an opportune time for sale or a commercially suitable time, one approach is to place the beneficiaries in funds through life assurance. For this purpose a joint life last survivor policy on the life of husband and wife could be considered.

5.42 Such a policy could be written in trust for the family so that it did not form part of the taxable estate. If this were done, each premium paid would represent a gift to the family. If there is income surplus to requirements then exemption for normal expenditure out of income could be claimed. Alternatively the premiums could be exempted by the annual inheritance tax exemption of £3,000 per annum. In addition to a policy which provided mainly life cover, an endowment policy could be used. This would give life cover, but the value of the policy would grow in value towards maturity date, so that there is also an investment element to this arrangement. Variations on this theme are possible such as funding monthly premiums into investment or unit trusts in the children's name or funding a Personal Equity Plan by monthly transfer taken out in their name.

5.43 If large lifetime gifts are made which qualify as potentially exempt transfers, life assurance can also be used to protect against death within seven years of making the gift. Commonly a seven-year term policy is used, where the sum assured is fixed for three years, and then reduces annually in line with the tapering of the tax liability described above.

Investing in assets that qualify for inheritance tax relief

5.44 Certain assets are favourably treated for inheritance tax purposes, with part or all of the value of the asset being exempt from tax. This applies particularly to certain business assets and to agricultural property.

Business property relief

5.45 Business property relief works by reducing the value of the asset subject to inheritance tax by either 50 per cent or 100 per

Estate Planning

cent, depending on the nature of the qualifying asset. Where the relief is 100 per cent the relief amounts to a complete exemption from inheritance tax. The assets which qualify and the amount of the relief given in each case is as follows.

Unquoted shares and securities (including loan stock)	100%
A business or interest in a business	100%
Quoted shares or securities which give control of the company	50%
Land, buildings, machinery or plant used for the business of a company controlled by the transferor	50%
Land, buildings, machinery or plant used by a partnership of which the transferor was a partner	50%
Land, buildings, machinery or plant held in a trust where the transferor is entitled to the trust income as of right and where the asset is used for a business which he carries on	50%

5.46 A business does not qualify for relief (and nor do shares or securities in a company carrying on such a business) if the business is not carried on for gain or is wholly or mainly:

- dealing in securities, stocks or shares;
- dealing in land or buildings;
- making or holding investments.

Exceptions are made for group holding companies, and United Kingdom based market makers and discount houses. Relief is also not available on land, buildings, machinery or plant used by a non-qualifying business.

5.47 If relief is to be obtained the following conditions must also be met:

- The asset must have been owned for a minimum two-year period. This can include earlier periods where property is replaced or inherited from a spouse.
- There must be no binding contract for the sale of the asset. (In the case of partnerships, the partnership

agreement should be reviewed to ensure this rule is not inadvertently breached.)
- In the case of company shares the company must not be in course of a winding-up, except where it is part of a reconstruction.

5.48 In valuing the assets which qualify for relief, any part which is attributable to excepted assets does not qualify for relief. Excepted assets are assets:

- not used wholly or mainly for the purpose of the business throughout the last two years prior to the transfer, or
- not required for future use for the purposes of the business at the time of the transfer, or
- assets used wholly or mainly for the personal benefit of the transferor or person connected with him.

5.49 In the case of lifetime gifts which are potentially exempt transfers, an occasion of charge to inheritance tax only arises if the donor dies within seven years of making the transfer. If this occurs relief on business property is only given if the donee has retained the asset throughout the period to date of death of the donee and it continues to qualify as business property. Relief is also given where the donee has replaced the original asset gifted with other business property.

5.50 In the case of farming businesses, land and buildings may also qualify for agricultural property relief. Where this is the case, agricultural property relief is given in priority and the asset is not then eligible for business property relief.

Agricultural property relief

5.51 Agricultural property relief is available in relation to assets consisting of agricultural land or pasture located in the United Kingdom, Channel Islands or the Isle of Man. It works by reducing the value of the asset subject to inheritance tax by either 50 per cent or 100 per cent, depending on the nature of the interest in the land. Like business property relief, where the relief is 100 per cent, the relief amounts to a complete exemption from inheritance tax. The amount of the relief applies as follows.

Land with vacant possession or the right to obtain it within 12 months	100%
Land owned, subject to a tenancy which begins after September 1, 1995	100%
Land which has been continuously held and tenanted since March 10, 1981 up to certain limits	100%
Other land interests, including a tenant's interest	50%

Agricultural land includes any buildings which are used for the intensive rearing of livestock or fish if occupied with the land and ancillary to it. It also includes farmhouses, cottages and farm buildings, together with the land occupied with them as are of a character appropriate to the property. Only the agricultural value qualifies for relief and if the land has development value this is excluded. **5.52**

No relief is given unless: **5.53**

- the transferor owns the property and occupies it himself for agricultural purposes for two years before the transfer; or
- the transferor owned the property for seven years before the transfer and throughout that period used the property, or let someone else use the property for agricultural purposes;
- there is *no* binding contract for the sale of the asset. (Again, in the case of partnerships, the partnership agreement should be reviewed to ensure this rule is not inadvertently breached.)

As with business property relief a clawback may occur if the donor dies within seven years of making a lifetime transfer. If this occurs relief is only given if the donee has retained the asset as agricultural property and it has been occupied for agricultural purposes throughout the period to date of death of the donor. Relief is also given where the donee has replaced the original asset gifted with other agricultural property. **5.54**

Gifts to grandchildren

5.55 One of the most effective gifts grandparents can make is to their minor grandchildren. The reason is that a minor child under the age of 18 is taxed in exactly the same way as an adult, *i.e.* he has a personal allowance for income tax and an annual exemption for capital gains tax, as well as all the lower rates of income tax. If parents try to take advantage of this, any income generated from funds they gift to their child in excess of £100 is aggregated with their own income and taxed as that of the parent (although capital gains are not so aggregated). No aggregation of income applies to funds gifted by grandparents.

5.56 Generally speaking it is unwise to make outright gifts to young children of large sums of money. A popular way of structuring gifts to grandchildren is to use an accumulation and maintenance trust. An accumulation and maintenance trust is a form of discretionary trust that has special exemptions from inheritance tax. It can be set up during lifetime or under a will. To qualify for the special treatment the terms of the trust must provide that one or more of the beneficiaries will become entitled to the trust assets, or to a liferent in them (*i.e.* the right to the income of the trust as it arises) on or before attaining a specified age of not more than 25. It is only the right to income that must be obtained by this age and capital can be held indefinitely or to a later age. Until then, income can either be accumulated or applied for the maintenance education or benefit of a beneficiary. Finally all the beneficiaries must be grandchildren of a common grandparent or not more than 25 years must have elapsed since the settlement commenced.

5.57 The advantages of an accumulation and maintenance trust are that gifts made to it are treated as potentially exempt transfers. There is no inheritance tax when capital is distributed from it to beneficiaries. Unlike other forms of discretionary trust, there are no inheritance tax charges at 10-year intervals.

5.58 For income tax purposes the trust is liable to income tax at a rate of 34 per cent. If the income is paid out to beneficiaries, and they are not taxpayers, the full 34 per cent can be recovered by the beneficiary. As an example, if an accumulation and maintenance trust receives gross income of £1,000 it will pay income tax of £340. This will leave the trustees £660 to distribute. The beneficiary is treated as receiving £1,000 gross with a tax credit of £340. If his personal allowance is available to offset the income he can obtain a tax repayment of £340 from the Inland Revenue.

5.59 A word of warning is required here. From April 6, 1999, dividend income of such a trust which is paid out to beneficiaries may incur an extra tax charge to compensate for the fact that the beneficiary will be able to recover the tax credit (unlike other individuals who cannot obtain repayment of tax credits on dividends). The effect of the extra tax charge on trustees is that dividend income which is distributed may suffer tax in the trustees' hands of 48.63 per cent. Equities may not necessarily be the best investment for such trusts in future unless income is to be accumulated and distributed as capital in future. Where the objective of the trust is to provide regular income to beneficiaries, a better choice of investment policy may be investments that do not pay dividends, such as fixed interest stocks or cash deposits. Capital gains tax is charged on trusts at a rate of 34 per cent and an annual exemption from capital gains tax is available, although this is usually one half of an individual's exemption (£3,400 for 1998/99) and may be less if more than one trust has been created on or after June 7, 1978 by the same settlor.

5.60 The trusts can be used to meet the cost of raising grandchildren, including meeting their education costs. Consultation with the parents is usually desirable before setting up such a trust, as it is a bad idea to leave the parents relatively badly off with the grandchildren wealthy. In very wealthy families where the children have their own inheritance tax problems an accumulation and maintenance trust can be used to skip a generation by passing wealth down to grandchildren on death. The children can do the same for their own grandchildren in due course of time with their own assets.

Gifts to charity

5.61 Many people are keen to benefit charity in their wills and during lifetime and there are many tax advantages which encourage this.

Gift aid

5.62 As an individual, a lifetime gift to charity in the form of a cash payment (including sums paid by cheque, bank transfer, or credit card) of a minimum lump sum of £250, where there are no significant benefits given in return, qualifies for a tax relief known as gift aid relief. The gift must be to a United Kingdom charity and gifts to foreign charities are not eligible.

5.63 The relief is best explained by an example.

Cash payment to a charity of	£10,000
This is treated as a gift net of basic rate tax of	£2,987
Making a gross total gift of	£12,987
Higher rate taxpayers are entitled to claim further tax relief of 40% less 23% basic rate	£2,208
The net of tax cost of making the gift is therefore	£7,792
The charity can reclaim the basic rate tax deducted so the value of the gift to the charity is	£12,987

5.64 The question of whether any significant benefits are received in exchange for the gift is important. A benefit is significant if it exceeds 2.5 per cent of the value of the gift subject to an overall ceiling of £250. Benefits paid to persons connected with the donor (which includes family and companies which he controls) are also prohibited. The Inland Revenue construe whether a benefit has been received very strictly.

5.65 It is important to ensure the donor has sufficient taxable income in any tax year ending on April 5, to cover the tax deducted from gift aid donations. If not, the basic rate tax must be paid to the Revenue.

Estate Planning

Deeds of covenant

Another way of making gifts tax-effectively to charity is by way of deed of covenant. Under a deed of covenant, a commitment is made to pay an annual sum for a period of at least four years. The payment is made net of basic rate tax and relief is given for higher rate tax in exactly the same way as shown in the example above for gift aid donations. There is no minimum to the amount which can be covenanted. **5.66**

Private charitable trusts

If charitable gifts of a substantial nature are intended, a private charitable trust or foundation can be used to good effect. Charitable purposes include the relief of poverty, the advancement of education, the advancement of religion and other purposes of a charitable nature beneficial to the community. Although the benefits are considerable the trust fund must be reasonably large to make the creation of a trust worthwhile. **5.67**

The features of a private trust are: **5.68**

- it affords flexibility in determining how and when charitable gifts will be spent;
- it can be used to receive legacies under a will, gift aid donations, gifts under deeds of covenant or gifts of assets such as shares at times and in amounts that suit the donor. The different causes to which distributions are to be made can be determined and paid later;
- the trust can continue to exist long into the future and after death of the donor.

Charitable trusts can be set up during lifetime. They are useful where it is intended to make lots of small one-off payments to charity of, say, £100 each which otherwise would not qualify for any form of tax relief. By making a large donation which enables the trust to recover tax there is a larger pot of money to benefit charities with. The private charity can also be formed on death by making provision in a will. The trust deed normally provides that payments of income and/or capital are to be made to charities or applied **5.69** for charitable purposes at the trustees' discretion. Normally this is broadly worded for maximum flexibility, but the terms and conditions applying can be modified to suit. In both cases the gift to the charity is exempt from inheritance tax and the trust itself suffers no charge to inheritance tax.

5.70 The deed forming the trust will appoint trustees to run it. The trust is controlled by its trustees which can include the settlor or his family, or could include professional advisers. The beneficiaries are determined by the trustees within overall parameters specified in the trust deed.

5.71 Once the trust is established an application is made for it to receive formal recognition as a charity. In Scotland this is made to the Inland Revenue, who will also confirm it has charitable status for tax purposes. It is then allocated a charity number and can begin receiving donations.

5.72 The trust is supervised by the Scottish Charities office. There are requirements for the trust to keep proper books of account and to produce annual statutory accounts which are required to disclose certain information including details of donations paid. Once a year the accounts must be submitted to the Inland Revenue.

5.73 Most income of the charity is exempt from tax and in the case of investment income, tax deducted at source can be reclaimed from the Inland Revenue. Basic rate tax on gift aid donations and on payments under deed of covenant can also be reclaimed. Currently Revenue practice is to accept claims for repayment at regular intervals during the course of the year rather than at the end. As a result funds accumulated within the trust are free of tax and to the extent not distributed in any year can be reinvested so that growth builds up quicker on the gross fund. There is no requirement for any minimum sum to be applied in any year and the trust can legitimately accumulate funds for quite some time. However, the funds must eventually be applied to a charitable purpose and if too little is distributed or no distributions are ever made the Inland Revenue would ultimately question tax relief due to the trust.

The trust is not liable to capital gains tax, provided the gains are applied for charitable purposes. In addition assets pregnant with gains can be gifted free of capital gains tax to the charitable trust. If realised within the trust the gains are tax free. This can be used to considerable advantage. For example, assume shares worth £100,000 are owned on which there is a capital gain of £80,000. If the shares were sold and cash gifted to the trust capital gains tax of about £32,000 might be paid. Instead the shares could be gifted to the trust, involving no payment of capital gains tax and the trust could sell them free of tax, thus securing gross funds of £100,000. 5.74

Overall strategy

Deciding on a strategy of giving away assets during lifetime is always a balance between reducing the tax liability and ensuring enough is retained to live on comfortably. In general assets that produce little or no income in preference to high income producing assets should be the subject of lieftime gifts. Annual exemptions should be used regularly, preferably at the start of each tax year, and other exemptions when the occasion arises, *e.g.* gifts on marriage. 5.75

Outright gifts are usually to be preferred as they involve no additional costs. Sometimes an outright gift may not be desirable. In these circumstances consider making gifts in trust. Trusts are particularly suitable for making gifts to young beneficiaries and in due course may be suitable for providing for grandchildren in a tax-efficient manner. 5.76

Chapter 6

STATE PROVISION FOR OLD AGE

The state pension

6.1 The earliest version of state provision of pension dates from 1908. At that time average life expectancy was 45 for a man and 49 for a woman. Today average life expectancy is 74 for a man and 79 for a woman. As we all live longer with life expectancy increasing in the next century, and as the working population shrinks leaving fewer people to support more in retirement there are increasing concerns about whether the state pension can be afforded in the years ahead.

6.2 The reason why this should be so stems from the fact that the existing state pension is funded by the contributions of the working population today, not on contributions made over the working life of the pensioner. The Government intends to put forward proposals for "stakeholder pensions" in the near future, but for those at the end of their working life the state scheme in its present form is likely to provide a safety net of income for the future. The extent of the safety net is in doubt and on some projections the state pension will be worth just 7 per cent of national average earnings by 2030.

6.3 At present the state pension age is 65 for men and 60 for women, but pension ages are to be equalised. This will be achieved over a 10-year period starting on April 6, 2010. The way it is to be achieved is to extend the age at which women qualify to age 65. Women born before April 6, 1950 will continue to reach pension age at 60 but women born after April 6, 1955 will not reach pension age until age 65. Those born in between will be entitled to pension at age 60 plus one month for each whole month or part of a month that their birthday falls after April 5, 1950. For example, a woman born on January 31, 1954 (three years and ten months after April 5, 1950) will be entitled to pension from November 6, 2017 when she is nearly 64.

6.4 To qualify for any state pension sufficient national insurance contributions must have been paid during working life. The working life starts at age 16 and normally finishes at state retirement age. The full basic state pension is paid if sufficient of the tax years in the working life are qualifying years. In a working life of over 41 years, at least 36 qualifying years are required. A qualifying year is, broadly, one in which either an amount equal to 52 class 1 contributions at the lower earnings limit or 52 class 2 or class 3 contributions or 52 credited contributions are shown on the individual's national insurance record. Class 1 contributions are paid by employees while class 2 contributions are paid by the self-employed. A reduced pension is paid if the requisite number of qualifying years are not met subject to a *de minimis* requirement of one-quarter. If the record is insufficient (*e.g.* because of a period working abroad) it can be made up by payment of voluntary class 3 contributions. Credited contributions are given in special circumstances such as absence through sickness. The easiest way to check entitlement is to apply (using Form BR 19) to the DSS at Newcastle-upon-Tyne who can supply a copy of the contribution record.

6.5 In addition to the basic state pension an earnings-related element "SERPS" is paid to those who have paid class 1 contributions since April 6, 1978. This limits the "SERPS" element to employees and it is not available to the self-employed. Not all employees are entitled to the "SERPS" element—those who are "contracted out" and pay national insurance contributions at the contracted-out level do not earn any earnings-related pension on these contributions, but they can only contract out if they have alternative pension arrangements. The amount of the "SERPS" element of pension is being amended for those reaching state retirement age or becoming widowed after April 6, 2000.

Prior to the introduction of SERPS in April 1975 a graduated pension was payable to those who paid graduated national insurance contributions. Those who have preserved rights to a graduated pension receive an increased amount of state pension. **6.6**

The state pension is not affected by the receipt of other earnings. It can be deferred by up to five years in which case a higher amount is paid. However, as the pension is paid for the life of the recipient only there is usually little merit in deferring receipt. **6.7**

A married woman can claim pension based on her own contributions when she reaches retirement age. Alternatively, if her husband has reached state retirement age and is in receipt of pension, she can claim a state retirement pension on his record. Married women's pension is paid at a lower rate than the full rate. Husband and wife are taxed on their own pension irrespective of whose contributions are used to arrive at the amount due. **6.8**

On the death of her husband after she reaches state retirement age, a widow can claim a retirement pension based on her late husband's record. Should he die before that age entitlement is to widow's pension. **6.9**

If an individual continues to work after having reached state retirement age, no national insurance contributions on earnings are paid. **6.10**

Social security benefits

As well as a state pension the British social security system provides a number of benefits for those who either have insufficient income or who are too infirm to care for themselves. The rules surrounding entitlement to benefit and the amount payable in each case are complex and are not covered in detail below. Those benefits which are particularly relevant to the elderly, however, are outlined and further information should be sought on any that appear relevant. There are many other benefits not mentioned, some **6.11** of which will be relevant in particular cases or for those caring for the elderly, and the details below should not be considered to be comprehensive of state support.

6.12 Many elderly people have low incomes which are not adequate to live on. Those who are over 60 and who work less than 16 hours a week may qualify for income support provided their partner, if any, works less than 24 hours a week. To qualify for income support, income and capital must not exceed prescribed limits. In the case of income, the amount of income support paid is calculated according to individual circumstances, but is the amount required to top income from all sources up to the level of a basic personal allowance. The elderly can expect that basic allowance to be increased by a pensioner premium. This premium starts at age 60 to age 74, rises to an enhanced pensioner premium from age 75 to 79 and finally a higher pensioner premium is paid to those over age 80. Those under 80 in receipt of certain other social security benefits such as attendance allowance, disability living allowance, mobility supplement, severe disablement allowance, registered blind, etc., may also receive this premium. Other premiums may be applicable. In addition the benefit may include an element to meet housing costs such as mortgage interest.

6.13 Income support is reduced if capital exceeds £3,000 in value and no support is given if capital exceeds £8,000. In calculating this figure the value of the principal residence is disregarded. Any personal possessions such as house contents, cars, etc., are also disregarded unless the item was acquired with the intention of reducing capital in order to qualify for higher benefits.

6.14 If income support is received it is income subject to income tax in the normal way. If income support is due the claimant will automatically be entitled to housing benefit. Housing benefit is paid by the local council to assist people to meet any rent they are due to pay for their home. The capital which may be held before entitlement to housing benefit is lost is raised to £16,000 but capital of between £3,000 and £16,000 will affect the amount of housing benefit due. For certain people living permanently in residential care homes or nursing homes the lower capital limit is raised to £10,000. Tenants of rented property who do not receive income support may also qualify for housing benefit if they satisfy a means test.

6.15 Council tax benefit may also be payable to reduce any council tax bills due. This is a social security benefit which is run by the local council. It is available to both home owners and those who rent property. A claim to council tax benefit will often be made at the same time as a claim to income support and is also a means-tested benefit. The maximum benefit is 100 per cent of the council tax excluding water charges and the benefit is usually deducted from the council tax bill when it is issued.

6.16 As people age they become more vulnerable to illness and disability which leaves them unable to care for themselves. For those aged 65 or over who need help with personal care in these circumstances, a claim for attendance allowance can be made. Attendance allowance is available to anyone over 65 and is not means-tested or dependent on national insurance contributions. The only requirement is that the claimant must have needed help with personal care for six months or more. In the case of a terminal illness the claims process is designed to give benefit quickly and easily without waiting for the six months care period to have elapsed.

6.17 Should the claimant require to go into hospital or residential care the level of benefits paid is usually reduced in view of the free care provided by the National Health Service. The local authority may also contribute to the cost. If income support is being paid it will include a residential allowance to help meet accommodation costs of a residential care home or nursing home. After four weeks attendance allowance may be withdrawn.

6.18 Leaflets which give more information on benefits available, the rates of benefit and how to claim them are available from local benefits agencies and many are also available in post offices.

6.19 As the level of capital which can be retained before entitlement to income support is quite low, many elderly people worry that their savings will be eroded if they have to go into residential care. Once many people assumed that if they could not care for themselves they would be admitted to hospital and cared for free of charge. Nowadays the National Health Service distinguishes between those who are ill and need medical care and those who are merely too frail to care for themselves but who are not ill, in deciding who to admit to hospital. Most health boards are planning for fewer long-term care beds for the elderly in the future and therefore fewer elderly people can be expected to be cared for free of charge in hospital than has been the case in the past. More places in residential homes should be made available by the social services section of local councils to make up for this but at present provision of these places is lagging behind. Furthermore, social services provision has to be paid for, subject to means tests, while health care is free. Many people in the community have not made sufficient provision to meet the cost which these changes in approach require, in their plans for old age.

6.20 The problem is exacerbated by the fact that more people are living longer and are likely to need care. Family life is changing and the number of single people who are elderly is on the increase. Geographically many families may live too far away or have insufficient room to provide care or support for elderly relatives. Taking all these factors together demand for care facilities is outstripping supply.

6.21 The cost of residential care varies greatly according to whether it is run by the local authority or privately run. While no one wants to be a burden on the family, it is unlikely that state funding will be available to meet increasing demand. This means that most people should now consider whether they need to start planning to fund long-term care, and what options are available to them.

6.22 Some elderly people believe if they give their assets away to family, they will qualify for support in meeting care costs from their local authority. They are concerned that their home may have to be sold and the proceeds used to fund care until the capital is reduced to £16,000. Accordingly many look at gifting the house to their children. This is very dangerous as there is no security of tenure for the donor. Should the child become bankrupt, die or borrow on the security of the house and be unable to repay, the donor may find himself homeless. A family trust is often used to offer protection against these issues but there can be tax complications as the trust is one in which the settlor retains an interest. Among other things this can result in capital gains tax on the ultimate sale as well as inheritance tax on death.

6.23 A gift made in contemplation of going into a home, the aim of which is to divest the donor of assets so that social security benefits can be claimed, may be ineffective. If made within six months of going into care the local authority can claim fees from the recipient. If made more than six months before going into care in theory the local authority can claim the fees from the donor as though the asset gifted was notional capital. The decision in *Yule v. South Lanarkshire Council*[1] decided that there was no time-limit on how far back a council could go to reclaim fees against gifts of assets.

6.24 There is a growing need for solutions to the cost of financing long-term care, and to meet this need the insurance industry is developing new products. These are in their infancy, which makes it difficult to judge whether they represent good value in meeting the needs of the people who buy them, especially as these needs are complex to judge. Although these products are developing rapidly and hence there are many variations, they fall into two broad categories—prefunded and point of need. In both cases the cost of long-term care cover is expensive and as most people do not know if they are ever going to need to draw on the cover, many are reluctant to take out insured products.

6.25 How should the question of long-term care needs be evaluated? The first issue is to work out what long-term care would cost. This varies from region to region according to

---

[1] [1998] S.L.T. 490.

what provision and financial assistance is given by the local authority and what private facilities are available. A weekly cost of between £350 to £500 upwards can be expected for full-time residential care. Care in the home can be even more expensive depending on what is required.

6.26 The second issue is to consider what additional personal expenses will continue after the individual goes into care. Different issues arise for married couples and single individuals as the latter may well sell their home and reduce expenditure considerably. The former may look at care in the home as an alternative to residential care and needs will be different. Personal expense may not fall significantly. Once the level of ongoing expense has been struck, a requirement for total weekly expenditure can be arrived at. From this requirement, net of tax income should be deducted to arrive at the shortfall that represents the funding need. Bear in mind that if capital is less than £10,000 full state assistance will be obtained with scaled-down assistance if capital is between £10,000 and £16,000, as explained above. Once the shortfall is calculated the alternatives to meet it can be considered.

6.27 The first approach involves paying regular premiums to an insurance company. At the point of need for care, the premiums cease and the amount covered by the policy (which should be the forecast shortfall) is paid by the insurance policy. Most policies do not pay out unless there is a need for care, which is established by setting a number of daily living tasks. Only if the individual covered cannot manage these without assistance is benefit paid.

6.28 The second approach involves making a lump-sum payment into either an investment-linked product or a protection policy. Often the cover provided by such an arrangement is subject to periodic review. However, those plans that are investment-linked may offer a recovery of capital if no claim is made for long-term care provision.

6.29 It is very difficult to be accurate about the funding requirement for long-term care ahead of the need arising, yet if there is a delay until the need is known the individual may be uninsurable or the cost too great.

A third approach is to use capital resources currently available as required. The danger here is that the capital runs out before the need to fund care stops and the individual becomes destitute. This approach therefore needs careful evaluation of life expectancy, capital resources and the effect on income of depleting these resources. The plan should take the impact of tax, especially capital gains tax, into account. Not all capital assets are necessarily liquid and the obvious example is the home. There are a number of approaches to accessing the value of the home to release capital which do not necessarily involve disposing of the home.

6.30

One type of approach is known as the shared appreciation mortgage. A loan is taken out on the value of the property but no interest is payable on this. Instead the lender shares in any growth in value of the property over which the loan is secured. So if a loan of £25,000 is taken out on a house worth £75,000, when the house is sold on death, one third of any increase in value over £75,000 plus the loan is repaid from the proceeds. There are risks to this arrangement. If other family members live in the house, selling it on death to repay the loan may leave them homeless. The release of cash from the property in the form of the loan may impact on social security benefits and contribution to care costs so it becomes self-defeating. Care is required that any such arrangements add to available resources and do not just replace state funding.

6.31

Other home income plans are available. The original home income plan is now discredited. In principle it involved remortgaging the house and using the proceeds to invest in unit-linked investment bonds. The return on the bond was intended to exceed the new borrowing cost, thus increasing the income available. With hindsight the high-risk nature of this arrangement can be seen. If interest rates rose and the investment return fell, the mortgage became unaffordable. Similarly if property prices fell, the loan could exceed the value of the house. This was exactly what happened in the

6.32

1980s but the lessons learned from the experience have given rise to new safer forms of home income plan. If these are considered it is wise to approach only members of the trade association SHIP (safe home income plans) in the first instance. SHIP is a collective initiative of the main providers of such schemes and its members must adhere to a strict code of practice.

6.33 There are two types of plan available. The first is a reversionary plan whereby all or part of the house is sold at a discount to its current value. The consideration is split into rent-free occupancy for life, plus a lump sum or an annuity income. The proportion of the home sold (between 30 per cent and 100 per cent) will depend on the funding requirement. The vendor will not share in any rise in value of the property in the part sold. Obviously if the lump sum is invested in an annuity this too will terminate on death and the capital will be lost to the estate. The risk is that the annuity will not meet rising future costs, so this plan should only be considered for older lives who benefit from higher annuity rates.

6.34 The second type is known as the mortgage annuity scheme. A fixed-rate mortgage subject to a maximum of £30,000, or 75 per cent of the property value if lower, is taken out. This is used to buy an annuity, part of which goes to pay the interest on the mortgage while the balance provides extra income to the annuitant. On death the property is sold and the mortgage repaid. By limiting the amount of the mortgage, the risk of negative equity if house prices fall is reduced. As the mortgage is based on fixed interest rates and the annuity rate is fixed at the outset, there is protection against falls in investment return and rises in interest rates. Nevertheless the benefit of this plan must be carefully weighed up. If interest rates are particularly high or annuity rates very low the economic benefit may be limited.

6.35 In any scheme involving a loan secured on the home, relief from tax for the interest cost should not be forgotten. If the loan is taken out as part of a scheme under which 90 per cent of the loan proceeds are used in purchasing a life annuity secured over the main residence, and either the loan is made to a person over the age of 65, or the annuitants had each attained 65, interest paid on the loan is eligible for relief. Relief is given as an income tax reduction, but unlike normal mortgage interest relief, the rate of relief is the basic rate of tax, currently 23 per cent. If the annuitant moves out of the home permanently, relief is lost but there is a 12-month period of grace in which to sell the home which the Inland Revenue can use their discretion to extend.

6.36 In the case of all these plans, it should be remembered that capital is being used up to fund the cost of care. That capital will be lost to the estate on death. As this reduces the amount that the heirs to the estate, typically children, will inherit, it is always worth involving them in the planning so that they understand what is intended and why. In some cases they may be willing to put up alternative funding and take on some of the risks so that any "profit" on the arrangements stays in the family and does not accrue to third parties. In that case care needs to be taken that all transactions are at market value if inheritance tax issues are not to arise.

6.37 While selling the house that is the principal private residence does not give rise to any capital gains tax charge, it will not be the principal private residence of the purchaser. On disposal after death, there will be capital gains tax payable on any gain realised (subject to taper relief if any). This is in contrast to the position if the property was wholly owned until death when there would be a tax-free uplift to market value at date of death which probably means that no tax would be payable on sale. In addition, the sale of property attracts stamp duty.

6.38 There is an exception to the capital gains tax charge in relation to property which is occupied by a dependent relative of the owner on a rent-free basis. The exception applies only to property which was owned on April 6, 1988 and occupied by the dependent relative on that date. The exemption from capital gains tax for a property, which is a principal private residence, can then be applied to this property as well as to the owner's own home. "Dependent relative" means, in relation to an individual, any relative of his or of his wife who is incapacitated by old age or infirmity from maintaining himself. It also includes his or his wife's mother who, whether or not incapacitated, is either widowed, or living apart from her husband, or a single woman in consequence of dissolution or annulment of marriage.

6.39 In conclusion, state support should be considered a safety net. It cannot be relied upon to provide for all needs in old age and where income is insufficient to meet these needs, contingency plans should be prepared to top up state support. The earlier such plans are made the better but there is a cost involved which is not insubstantial. Lack of certainty over future requirements, if any, make this a complex area and decisions should not be made lightly.

Chapter 7

DEATH

No one likes to consider their own death, yet making plans for this can substantially ease matters for family at a time when the distress of bereavement can make it hard to cope. **7.1**

A simple step is to prepare a list of documents and other information that the executors of the estate will require to wind it up. The list should also contain other information on matters that may require immediate action following death. The Institute of Chartered Accountants of Scotland has produced an Organiser which details the type of information that should be included in this list and this is reproduced in the Appendix. **7.2**

Death is not the only occasion that this information can be vital. Sadly, an increasing number of people are affected by Alzheimer's disease or other diseases causing senility in old age. Those afflicted can reach the stage when they are unable to manage their own affairs. This can have the horrendous consequence that just at the time finances need to be rearranged and assets sold to provide for extra care, the individual affected may lack the capacity to carry out these transactions. An effective solution to this concern is to grant a power of attorney at a time when the individual has the capacity to make decisions. **7.3**

A power of attorney gives someone the power to act on behalf of the individual granting it. On production of the deed granting the power of attorney, the attorney can sign documents, sell assets, operate bank accounts and do anything else specified in the document just as though he was the individual **7.4** himself. It is commonly used, for example, by someone moving abroad for a short period of time, and it operates for the time specified in the deed or until withdrawn by the person granting it. Powers of attorney granted before January 1, 1991 lapse if the grantor becomes incapacitated mentally. Powers of attorney granted on or after that date remain in force if the grantor becomes incapacitated unless the terms of the power granted stipulate to the contrary.

7.5 The person being granted the power of attorney is given very wide powers and in consequence it should be someone trusted implicitly by the grantor. It need not be just one person—joint powers of attorney are common. Since it may not come into effect until many years after being granted it is an idea to list various alternative attorneys since the first choice may not be able to act. In selecting the person or persons to be granted the power of attorney it is important to remember that the choice must be practical as documents may have to be signed quickly. Normally the powers granted are fully comprehensive and will enable the person granted the power to do virtually anything the grantor could do if he had the capacity. Like a will, a power of attorney can be changed at any time before it comes into operation.

7.6 It is not just old age that can render a person unable to act and the best time to prepare a power of attorney is at the same time as a will is being drawn up. This ensures that incapacity as the result of an accident or a stroke or other illness will also be covered.

7.7 Everyone should have a will. First and foremost a will directs how your estate will be divided after death. Secondly, it appoints executors who take responsibility for ingathering the estate, paying inheritance tax due and transferring the title to assets to those who inherit the estate. Without a will it is necessary to go to court to appoint executors and this process adds expense and time to that needed to wind up an estate.

7.8 Not all assets will be covered by the will. Jointly owned assets may be covered by a special destination as a result of which they pass to the joint owner automatically on the first to die. This commonly applies to the joint title to a house. It may also apply to bank and building society accounts.

7.9 A will can, of course, be changed at any time during lifetime either by completely rewriting it or by adding a codicil to it. There are dangers in trying to write a will without the professional help of a solicitor. Some stationers stock pro forma wills which simply require blanks to be filled in. The problem is that many of these pro formas are designed under English law and the substantial differences in Scots law in this area can result in the pro forma being both incomplete or, worse, invalid. It is very easy to draft a will that is ambiguous in its meaning or which does not cover the entire estate leaving part to fall under the law of intestacy. For that reason it is advisable to seek the professional help of a solicitor.

7.10 The terms of a will may be changed in two other circumstances after death. First, they can be overruled by a legal rights claim. Secondly, the beneficiaries under the will can enter into a deed of variation under which by agreement they redirect the destination of assets.

Succession

7.11 If the deceased dies without leaving a will, a widow or widower has certain "prior rights" in the estate, irrespective of what other relatives survive the deceased. The surviving spouse is entitled to:

- the dwelling-house in which the surviving spouse was resident at the time of the death up to a value of £110,000 for deaths on or after November 26, 1993 (in certain cases, *e.g.* where the house is a farmhouse or is worth more than £110,000, the entitlement is not to the house itself but to its value up to £110,000);
- the furniture in the house, up to a value of £20,000; and
- if there are no children or remoter issue—cash amounting to £50,000, rateably from the remainder of the estate, after the housing and furniture rights have been satisfied, *or*

- if there are children or remoter issue—cash amounting to £30,000, rateably from the remaining estate after the housing and furniture rights have been satisfied.

Legal rights

7.12 After prior rights have been taken, a surviving widow/widower, and children/issue have certain legal rights in the moveable estate of a deceased. The moveable estate includes cash and investments but excludes any land and buildings which are classed as heritable property.

7.13 The surviving spouse is entitled to one-third of the deceased's moveable estate if the deceased left children, or to one-half if no such children were left.

7.14 The children are entitled to one-third of the deceased's moveable estate if the deceased left a spouse, or to one-half of it if the deceased left no spouse, divided equally between them.

7.15 Subject to these prior rights of the spouse, and to a claim for legal rights, the following persons inherit the balance of the estate, often called the dead's part, absolutely.

(1) If there are children of the deceased living at the date of death they share the balance equally. If a child has predeceased the deceased, his or her children (or remoter issue), if any, take their parent's share of the estate, divided among such grandchildren equally.

If there are no children or remoter issue the following people inherit the balance of the estate in the following order:

(2) Mother/father and brothers and sisters—half to parent or parents and half to brothers and sisters. Where the deceased is an illegitimate child then the whole estate goes to parent or parents.

(3) If there are no parents then brothers and sisters take the whole.

(4) Either or both parents take the whole if there are no brothers and sisters.

(5) Failing parents and siblings, uncles or aunts (on either parent's side) take the whole.
(6) Grandparent or grandparents (on either side) take the whole.
(7) Brothers and sisters of any grandparents (on either side) take the whole.
(8) Ancestors of the intestate remoter than grandparents, on both paternal and maternal sides, generation by generation successively take the whole, but if no ancestors survive in any generation their brothers or sisters come before ancestors of the next more remote generation.
(9) Failing any relatives in the foregoing categories, finally, the Crown as *"ultimus haeres"*, takes the whole.

Where a will is left, there is a choice of accepting the entitlement under the will or accepting the entitlement to legal rights. Both cannot be claimed. 7.16

A common assumption is that all assets pass to the surviving spouse on death. It can be seen from the foregoing that this is not true and it is desirable to make a will in many cases to achieve the desired distribution of the estate. Even then, this can be defeated in part by a legal rights claim as described above. Consider the following example: 7.17

A husband dies leaving a house worth £80,000, contents of £20,000 and investments worth £50,000. There is no will. His widow would be entitled to the house and contents, cash of £30,000 and one-third of the moveable estate remaining of £20,000, *i.e.* £6,667. His children would share the balance of £13,333. If he has left all his property to his wife under a will, his children could claim legal rights of one-third of the moveables of £70,000 (contents and investments) amounting to £23,333. In this situation, a will knocks out the prior rights of the spouse, and leaves a claim for legal rights to children that reduces the estate passing to the spouse below that which would pass if the deceased had died intestate. Apart from estates where the size makes this a trap, in most cases a will is desirable. 7.18

Deeds of variation

7.19 A deed of variation is an instrument which must be entered into in writing. It can be used either to alter the destination of assets as the beneficiaries decide among themselves or to disclaim a legacy. For tax purposes it must be made within two years of the date of death. On an election being made, the alteration is treated as though made by the deceased and inheritance tax is payable on that basis. An election must be made by written notice given to the Inland Revenue within six months after the date of the instrument, by the person or persons making the instrument (and, where the variation results in additional inheritance tax being payable, the personal representatives). The variation can decrease or increase the inheritance tax payable on the deceased's estate, but there is no transfer for inheritance tax purposes by the heirs. The tax treatment does not apply if any consideration is paid for the variation. A similar set of conditions apply for capital gains tax so that the redirection of assets is not treated as a disposal by the original legatee. The same time-limits for both the deed and the election apply. The elections for inheritance tax and capital gains tax are mutually exclusive and there is no requirement to make both.

7.20 A deed of variation is usually employed to take account of circumstances prevailing at the time of death which cannot be foreseen when the will is prepared. For example, a widow's income may be greater or less than anticipated and the family may redirect assets to and from the widow to compensate. Tax changes may have taken place since the will was signed which may have unexpectedly increased the tax burden and the deed of variation can be used to mitigate these.

7.21 It may be sensible for the will to leave all assets to the surviving spouse both to take advantage of the spouse exemption from inheritance tax and to ensure there is sufficient to provide for the surviving spouse. If the assets inherited exceed what the spouse requires there are two choices. A deed of variation can be entered into to redirect assets to children. This would be sensible if part of the nil rate band for inheritance tax had not been used. Alternatively the surviving spouse can accept the legacy and then make lifetime gifts to the family. These would be potentially exempt transfers which would be exempt from inheritance tax if the donor survived seven years from making the gift.

7.22 The reverse process of leaving assets in the will to the children is less sensible if there is a possibility the children will wish to redirect funds to the surviving spouse. First, if the estate exceeds the nil rate band, tax will be payable before confirmation to the estate can be obtained. Secondly, tax may be saved by using the deed of variation to redirect assets to the spouse to take advantage of the spouse exemption. If subsequently the spouse tries to make lifetime gifts back to the children, the gifts will be vulnerable to challenge by the Capital Taxes Office. When a deed of variation is made in favour of a spouse, before granting the spouse exemption, the Capital Taxes Office usually ask if any gifts to family are in contemplation. If such gifts back to the original beneficiaries are made, the Revenue will argue that the deed of variation is made for consideration representing the gift back, and in consequence the inheritance tax and capital gains tax elections are ineffective.

7.23 Sometimes the deceased person merely expresses a wish that property bequeathed by his will should be transferred by the legatee to other persons. If the legatee transfers any of the property in accordance with that wish within the period of two years after the death, inheritance tax is calculated as if the property transferred had been bequeathed by the will to the transferee.

7.24 Capital gains tax is not charged on death although the beneficiaries to the estate are deemed to inherit assets at market value as has been explained earlier. If the individual has sustained allowable losses in the year of assessment in which he dies, the losses may be deducted first from gains realised in the year and then from chargeable gains accruing to the deceased in the three preceding years of assessment. The executors to the estate have a capital gains tax annual exemption equivalent to the full exemption an individual has in the year of assessment in which he dies and in the two following tax years. If assets rise in value after death it can be worthwhile if the executors sell them and distribute cash to the legatee to take advantage of this exemption.

7.25 Inheritance tax and its predecessor, capital transfer tax, succeeded a death duty called estate tax. The spouse exemption for estate tax operated in reverse to the current exemption with relief being given on the second death. To take advantage of the estate duty exemption it was common for the will to leave assets in trust for the spouse who was entitled to a liferent of them. Where such a trust was created on the death of an individual before November 13, 1974 the trust assets are exempt from inheritance tax on the subsequent death of the spouse entitled to the liferent. It is important not to overlook this exemption for planning purposes.

7.26 After death has occurred, no one has title to the individual's assets. Effectively all assets are frozen until the executors' title is confirmed. In order to obtain confirmation, the executors must first prepare an inventory of all the assets and liabilities in the estate. The inventory is prepared on a form obtainable from the Capital Taxes Office (or in the case of small estates from the post office as well). The accuracy of the inventory must be attested to by the executors before a sheriff officer and any inheritance tax due must be calculated and paid before confirmation is obtained. This raises a problem for the executors. If assets are frozen, how can they raise the money to meet the tax due? This chicken and egg position is usually resolved by obtaining a bank loan until the title to the estate can be obtained and assets sold to realise sufficient cash.

7.27 Income tax relief is available to the executors for the loan interest payable within one year of the making of such a loan to pay inheritance tax on death. If the executors have insufficient income in that year to offset the loan interest, relief can be carried forward to a later year. Executors need to be careful that they take out a loan for this purpose and do not obtain an overdraft, as overdraft interest is not allowable for tax purposes.

7.28 The inventory to the estate must be completed and lodged with the Capital Taxes Office within 12 months of the end of the month in which death occurred. The tax payable on death is due for payment by the executors within six months of the end of the month in which death occurs. Individuals who have received lifetime gifts on which tax becomes payable on death (*i.e.* gifts made within seven years of death) must also pay tax due within six months of the end of the month in which death occurs. In practical terms because of the need to unfreeze assets tax is often paid before this deadline. If tax is paid later it carries interest from the date due.

7.29 The delay in obtaining title to the estate can create problems for the family. In particular a surviving spouse may have some time to wait before cash and income resources are released. As a precaution against this eventuality it is a good idea for couples to arrange their affairs so that each spouse has access to a reasonable liquid sum of cash in their own right. This can provide a bridge until the estate is administered.

7.30 Social security also provides some help. Anyone who is in receipt of income support, council tax benefit, housing benefit, income-based jobseekers allowance, family credit or disability working allowance and who can reasonably be expected to take responsibility for funeral costs may be able to obtain a funeral payment from the social fund to help with the cost. This is repayable out of any property left by the deceased but not otherwise.

Tax

7.31 On death, the executors are responsible for making tax returns of income and capital gains to the date of death and paying any tax due. It is quite often the case that income tax for the year of death is repayable as full personal allowances are available to set against income. This can mean that too much tax has been deducted from income which has been taxed at source, including pension income.

7.32 For capital gains tax purposes the executors are deemed to have the same residence, ordinary residence and domicile as the deceased at date of death, and for the estates of those affected this can mean that tax liabilities of the executors can be significantly reduced.

7.33 While the estate is being administered, income received by the executors is taxed at basic or lower rates depending on whether it is investment income or not. That income is also taxed on the beneficiaries entitled to the residue of the estate in the normal way with credit for the tax paid by the executors. This is achieved by treating any payment made to the beneficiaries as income, up to the level of income received by the estate to date (including income carried forward from earlier tax years if not already attributed to a beneficiary). A payment can include a payment of cash, assets such as furniture, or other capital transferred in kind. Once the income of the executry received by the executors to date is exhausted, any future income received by the executors is taxed on the beneficiary up to the level of the balance of the payment he received. Ultimately this system means that when the whole estate is distributed, all the income of the executry will have been taxed on the beneficiaries but not necessarily in the same tax year in which it arose. The executors pay tax on capital gains in excess of any annual exemption at a rate of 34 per cent.

7.34 If a beneficiary is liable to higher rate tax on income he receives from an executry, and that income has been reflected in the value of assets which were subject to inheritance tax at date of death, relief is given for inheritance tax against the income tax liability. This relief is often overlooked. Where the spouse exemption has operated so that no inheritance tax is payable on death, no relief will be due so it does not apply to widows or widowers. Equally no relief is available if the beneficiaries are not higher rate taxpayers, or the taxable estate falls below the nil rate band. In the remaining cases, as well as income accrued at date of death, dividends may be received by the executry many months after death that were declared to be payable in respect of accounting periods ending prior to death. This dividend income qualifies for relief. In each case the average inheritance tax rate applicable to the estate is applied to the net of tax income received in working out the relief due.

7.35 A widow is granted a widow's bereavement allowance as described in Chapter 1 in the year of her husband's death and in the following year to reduce her income tax liability. It is common for a widow to be entitled to a widow's pension following her husband's death and entitlement to state pension may also change. To avoid paying too much or too little tax it is important for the widow to notify the Inland Revenue of the changes as soon as possible so that any Notice of Coding can be amended at an early date.

7.36 Each stage of the lifecycle brings its own financial challenges. For the elderly it is the uncertainty over how much funding will be required, and for how long it will be required, that complicates matters in planning their affairs. By taking time to understand the opportunities available and plan the whole financial picture, the elderly will improve their chances of enjoying this period of their lives without financial worries, and of passing on their affairs in good order to the next generation.

Appendix

ESTATE ORGANISER

WHERE TO FIND MY DOCUMENTS
– and other useful information

Name ....

Address ....

Date prepared ....

Contents
1. What you will need immediately
2. Details of my Will
3. My Life Assurance, Pension & Related Policies
4. My Home
5. My Business/Employment
6. My Car
7. My Property and Investments
8. My Bank and Similar Accounts
9. My Plastic Cards, Loans and Liabilities
10. My Tax Details
11. My Professional Advisers
12. Other Information

NOTE
This record is intended to facilitate the location of important documents and information in the event of death or incapacity. It must not be regarded as a substitute for a proper Will. Its only purpose is to address the practical difficulties of coping with financial queries at a time when close relatives may be distressed.

It is suggested that a spouse/adult child is made aware of the existence/ location of this record and/or a copy should be given to a close relative/ executor as a precaution against a common calamity.

1. WHAT YOU WILL NEED IMMEDIATELY

a. My deed/safe box may be found:

....

The key is kept: ....

And the key number is: ....

b. I have/do not have a private healthcare policy with:

....

This is/is not a company scheme.

The policy document may be found:....................

c. My Birth/Marriage and similar Certificates may be found:

....

d. I do/do not have a lair.

The deeds may be found:....................................

e. My Clergyman is   My Doctor is:

Name...........................   Name...............................

Address........................   Address............................

....

Telephone: ....   Telephone: ....

2. MY WILL

The original of my Will is held by/may be found in:

....

....

A copy may be found in:

....

....

It is dated: ....

There is no Codicil/Codicils are dated:

....

The Will was prepared by: ....

Address: ....

            ....

            ....

Telephone: ....

Executor(s) to my Will is/are: ....

....

3. MY LIFE ASSURANCES, PENSION AND RELATED POLICIES

My life assurances, pensions, disability and personal accident policies etc. are listed below:

Company	Policy No.	Life Covered	Purpose	Document Location

4. MY HOME

My principal residence is at ....

....

....

I am sole/joint owner with..

Mortgate with   ....

Address   ....

                ....

                ....

Telephone   ....

Mortgage reference number..

Title deeds placed with ....

Buildings insurance cover with..

and policy may be found...

Home contents insurance cover with.....................................

and policy may be found...

5. MY BUSINESS/EMPLOYMENT

I am owner of/partner in ....

Address ....

....

Telephone ....

Contact name ....

Home Telephone number ....

Keys to business premises may be found

....

I am employed by ....

Address ....

....

Contact name ....

Telephone ....

Payroll/works number ....

I am/am not a member of a company pension scheme.

Scheme documentation may be found ....

Death in service benefit does not apply/aplies at a level of

....

List of Directorships ....

6. MY CAR

My car is/is not a company vehicle.

The registration document/MOT cerficiate may be found

....

The car is insured with..

Address   ....

....

Telephone   ....

The insurance certificate may be found   ....

The insurance policy may be found   ....

The car is/is not subject to an HP/Finance/Loan Agreement with

....

Address   ....

....

Telephone   ....

The Agreement may be found

....

....

7. MY PROPERTY & INVESTMENTS

I am the sole/joint owner with ....

of property/timeshare/caravan at ....

....

....

Loan/mortgage with ....

Address ....

....

Telephone ....

Loan/mortgage reference number ....

Title deeds with/may be found ....

The asset is/is not let commercially to ....

....

Lease/other documentation may be found ....

....

My investment register/schedule of investments may be found

....

....

My investment certificates may be found

....

....

8. MY BANK AND SIMILAR ACCOUNTS

I have the following accounts with the Banks and financial institutions stated.

Bank Name ....

Address ....

....

Telephone ....

	Type of Account	Account No.	Sole/Joint With
1			
2			
3			

Bank Name ....

Address ....

....

Telephone ....

	Type of Account	Account No.	Sole/Joint With
1			
2			
3			

Bank Name ....

Address ....

....

Telephone ....

	Type of Account	Account No.	Sole/Joint With
1			
2			
3			

8a. MY BANK AND SIMILAR ACCOUNTS (CONTINUED)

I have standing order/direct debit arrangements as noted below:

Bank	Account No.	Payee	Purpose

9. MY PLASTIC CARDS, LOANS AND LIABILITIES

I have the following plastic cards:

Issuer	Telephone No.	Card No.	Expiry Date

I keep these in my wallet/purse. They can be found

....

I have the following loans/liabilities not included elsewhere in this document.

Lender	Account No.	Repayment Terms	Completion Date

Documentation may be found

....

10. MY TAX DETAILS

My tax office is ....

Address ....

....

....

Telephone ....

Reference No. ....

National Insurance No. ....

For inheritance tax purposes details of gifts made are held by my accountant/solicitor or are detailed below:

Date	Asset	Donee

11. MY PROFESSIONAL ADVISERS

My professional advisers are:

Solicitor ....

Address ....

....

Telephone ....

Accountant ....

Address ....

....

Telephone ....

Other ....

Address ....

....

Telephone ....

12. OTHER INFORMATION

This section can be used to provide supporting information for items on earlier pages, *e.g.* schedule of investments, or to list other details such as membership of associations, clubs and societies, trusteeships, etc.

INDEX

abroad, pensioners living abroad, tax consequences, 1.46–49
accumulation and maintenance trusts, advantages, 5.57
  dividend income, 5.59
  gifts from grandparents, 5.56
  income tax, 5.58
  purposes, 5.60
advance corporation tax, purchase of own shares, 4.36, 4.37
age, allowances, 1.27–31, 3.81
  retirement, 3.1
  retirement relief, 4.19
  state pensions, 6.3
agricultural property, agricultural property relief, 5.50, 5.51–54
  clawbacks, 5.54
  holdover relief, 5.13
  meaning, 5.52
Alzheimer's disease, 7.3
annuities, *see also* **life annuities**
  calculation of income, 5.27
  mortgage annuity schemes, 6.34
  pensions, choice of options, 3.16–19
    equity-linked, 3.19
    impaired lives, 2.68
    joint annuities, 3.17
    open market option, 2.65
    options, 2.66
    PAYE, 1.5
    retirement annuities, 2.29, 2.35–40
    with-profit annuities, 2.68
attendance allowance, 6.16
  withdrawal, residential and hospital care, 6.17

blind person's allowance, 1.39
building societies, 3.24–27
  interest rates, 3.26–27
  investment risk, 3.24–25
  obsolete accounts, 3.27
  PIBS, 3.54
building society permanent interest bearing shares, 3.54
business property relief, 5.45–50
businesses, assets sale, 4.5, 4.8–10
  holdover relief, 5.13
  disposal, 4.1–44
    capital gains tax, 4.18–35
    connected persons, 4.8
    ex gratia payments, 4.39
    income tax, 4.8–17
      overlap relief, 4.13, 4.15
    meaning, 4.23
    sales as going concerns, 4.5
    strategy, 4.6
  forms, 4.2
  income from, estimation, 3.9
  income tax, 4.11
  succession, 4.40–42

capital, investment trusts, split capital, 3.70
  limits, help with residential care, 6.26
  income support, 6.13, 6.19
  notional capital, 6.23
  use to finance residential care, 6.30–38
capital allowances, disposal of assets, 4.14
capital bonds, National Savings, 3.46

capital gains tax, 3.75, 3.76–81
  businesses, disposal, 4.18–35
  deeds of variation, 7.19, 7.22
  disposal of assets, identification rules, 3.77
  effect of PETs, 5.10
  gifts between spouses, 1.35
  gilts, 3.48
  homes, dependent relatives, 6.38
    gifts to family trusts, 6.22
    home income plans, 6.37
  indexation allowance, 3.76
  investment trusts, 3.71
  legacies, 7.24
  losses, 3.80
  notification requirements, 1.11
  pension funds, 2.4
  PIBS, 3.54
  qualifying corporate bonds, 3.56
  reliefs, charities, 5.74
    enterprise investment scheme relief, 4.35
    executors, 7.24, 7.32
    holdover relief (*see* **holdover relief**)
    retirement relief (*see* **retirement relief**)
    rollover relief, 4.35
    taper relief, 3.78, 4.32
    transfer of assets between spouses, 3.81
    venture capital trust relief, 4.35
  returns, death, 7.31
  shares, 3.59
  trusts, 5.59
  unit trusts, 3.68
capital transfer tax, 7.25
Channel Islands, residents, income tax allowances, 1.47
charities, capital gains tax, 5.74
  charitable purposes, 5.67
  charitable trusts, 5.67–74
    Inland Revenue recognition, 5.71
    supervision, 5.72
    trustees, 5.70
  deeds of covenant, 5.66, 5.73

charities, *cont.*
  gifts, 5.29, 5.61–74
    gift aid relief, 5.62, 5.73
    income tax, 5.73
children, gifts, from grandparents, 5.55–60
  use of trusts, 5.56–57, 5.76
  legal rights, 7.12–18
codicils, 7.9
Commonwealth citizens, living abroad, income tax allowances, 1.47
companies, purchase of own shares, 4.36
  retirement of owners, 4.4
confirmation of executors, 7.26
council tax benefit, 6.15
Crown employees, living abroad, income tax allowances, 1.47

death, 7.1–36, *see also* **executors; inheritance tax; succession; wills**
  tax returns, 7.31
deeds of covenant, 5.66
deeds of variation, wills, 7.10, 7.19–21
directors, retirement relief, 4.25
discretionary trusts, lifetime gifts, holdover relief, 5.16
  inheritance tax, 5.6
  will planning, 5.37, 5.38
dividends, before sale of shares, 4.37
  income, 4.42
    accumulation and maintenance trusts, 5.59
    inheritance tax relief, 7.34
  taxation, 3.59, 3.74
division and sale, family homes, 5.34
documents, estate planning, 7.2

earnings cap, occupational pension schemes, 2.8
  personal pension schemes, 2.23, 2.35
  retirement annuity pensions, 2.27, 2.35
  unapproved retirement benefit schemes, 2.51

Index

emergencies, 3.22
enterprise investment scheme relief, 4.35
estate tax, 7.25
estates, *see also* **succession**
  capital gains tax, 7.32, 7.33
  income tax, 7.33
    higher rate, 7.34
  inventories, 7.26, 7.28
  moveable estates, legal rights, 7.12–14
  planning, 5.1–76
    documents, lists, 7.2
E.U. citizens, income tax allowances, 1.47
executors, appointment, 7.7
  capital gains tax, 7.32
  exemption, 7.24
  confirmation, 7.26
expenditure, retirement planning, 3.3, 3.11–15

farming, agricultural property relief, 5.50, 5.51–54
  retirement relief, disposal of business or assets, 4.23
funeral costs, social fund, 7.30
FURBS, 2.51–52
furniture, prior rights, 7.11

gift aid relief, 5.62
gifts, lifetime gifts (*see* **lifetime gifts**)
gilts, 3.47–53
  conversion, personal pension schemes, 2.45
  income tax deductions, 1.45
  index-linked, 3.48, 3.53
  interest payments, 3.52
  trading, 3.50
goodwill, 4.5, 4.18
  succession, 4.41
government securities, *see* **gilts**
grandparents, gifts to grandchildren, 5.55–60

heritable property, gifts, 5.29
holdover relief, 5.10, 5.11–18
  crystallisation, non-resident donees, 5.17

holdover relief, *cont.*
  gifts to discretionary trusts, 5.16
  restrictions, 5.14
home income plans, 6.31–36
homes, division and sale, 5.34
  gifts to family, effect on financing of residential care, 6.22–23
  joint ownership, tax implications, 5.33
  lifetime gifts, reservation of benefits, 5.20, 5.34
  prior rights, 7.11
housing benefit, 6.14

ill health, retirement relief, 4.30
income bonds, National Savings, 3.44
income support, 6.12–14
  capital limits, 6.13, 6.19
  income tax, 6.14
  pensioner premium, 6.12
  residential and hospital care, 6.17, 6.19–23
income tax, accumulation and maintenance trusts, 5.58
  age allowance, 1.27–31, 3.81
    income limit, 1.31
    married couples, 1.30
  blind person' allowance, 1.39
  businesses, disposal, 4.8–17
  capital allowances, disposal of assets, 4.14
  charities, 5.73
  codes (*see* **notices of coding**)
  estates, 7.33
    higher rate, 7.34
  estimates, 3.14
  gilts, 3.48
  income support, 6.14
  investment bonds, 3.58
  investment trusts, 3.71
  life annuities, 3.57
  non-pension income, 1.9
  non-tax-payers, investment income, 1.43–45
  overpayments, reasons, 1.1–3
  PAYE, 1.2
    pension annuities, 1.5

income tax, *cont.*
  pensioners living abroad, 1.46–49
  pensions, 1.4–21
  personal allowances, 1.23–26
  qualifying corporate bonds, 3.56
  rates, 1.42
  reliefs, medical insurance, 1.41
    mortgage relief, 6.35
    overlap relief, 4.13, 4.15
  repayments, 1.12
  returns, 1.13
    death, 7.31
  scope for errors, 1.32
  self-assessment (*see* **self-assessment**)
  tax deductions, 1.22–32
  underpayments, 1.14
  unit trusts, 3.68
  widow's bereavement allowance, 1.40
income tax planning, 1.33–49
  annuities, 1.34
  joint investments, 1.36–38
    declarations, 1.37
  married couples, 1.35
  tax-free investments, 1.33
individual savings accounts, *see* **ISAs**
inflation, life annuities, 3.57
  pension annuities, 3.18
  retirement planning, 3.3
inheritance tax, 5.2
  death in service benefits, 5.39–40
  deeds of variation, 7.19, 7.22
  discretionary trusts, 5.6, 5.37, 5.38
  funding through life insurance, 5.41–43
  interest, 7.28
  liferent trusts, 7.25
  lifetime gifts (*see* **lifetime gifts**)
  payment, 7.28
    loans, 7.26, 7.27
  potentiallly exempt transfers (*see* **PETs**)
  rates, 5.4, 5.7
  reliefs, 5.22–36
    against income tax liability, 7.34

inheritance tax, *cont.*
  agricultural property relief, 5.50, 5.51–54
  business property relief, 5.45–50
  spouses, 1.35, 5.30–36, 7.34
  taper relief, 5.5
  will planning, 5.37–38
insurance, financing long-term care, 6.24–28
  life assurance, funding inheritance tax, 5.41–43
  medical insurance, income tax relief, 1.41
interest, inheritance tax, 7.28
  late payment of tax, self-assessment, 1.15
  rates, building societies, 3.26–27
investment bonds, 3.58
  income tax, 1.34, 3.58
  unit-linked, home income plans, 6.32
investment trusts, 3.69–72
  split capital, 3.70
    income tax, 1.34
investments, choices, 3.20–73
  collective investments, 3.66
  income, gross payment, 1.43–45
  liquidity, 3.21, 3.22
  pensions and alternatives, comparisons, 2.50
  retirement income, estimation, 3.8
  risk, 3.23
ISAs, 1.33, 2.47, 3.35–37
  annual limits, 3.35
  CAT standards, 3.37
  investment routes, 3.36
  transfer of TESSAs, 3.37
Isle of Man, residents, income tax allowances, 1.47

joint investments, income tax planning, 1.36–38
joint ownership, special destinations, 5.33, 7.8

legacies, capital gains tax, 7.24
  disclaiming, 7.19

Index

legal rights, 5.36, 7.12–18
  dead's part, 7.15
  overruling wills, 7.10
  wills or legal rights, 7.16
life annuities, 3.57
  income tax, 1.34, 3.57, 3.58
life assurance, bonds, single premium (*see* **investment bonds**)
  funding inheritance tax, 5.41–43
liferent trusts, 5.3, 7.25
lifetime gifts, *see also* **PETs**
  between spouses, capital gains tax, 3.81
  income tax planning, 1.35
  homes to family trusts, tax implications, 6.22
  inheritance tax, 5.4, 5.5
    discretionary trusts, 5.6
    exemptions, 5.22–36
    payments, 7.28
    strategy, 5.75–76
    to charities, 5.29, 5.61–74
    to grandchildren, 5.55–60
liquidity, choice of investments, 3.21, 3.22
loans, payment of inheritance tax, 7.26, 7.27

maintenance, payments, inheritance tax, 5.29
marriage, *see also* **spouses**
  gifts in anticipation, 5.29
married women, state pensions, 6.8
medical insurance, income tax relief, 1.41
mortgages, home income plans, 6.32–36
  mortgage annuity schemes, 6.34
  shared appreciation mortgages, 6.31

national insurance contributions, after retirement age, 6.10
  state pensions, 6.4
National Savings, 3.38–46
  capital bonds, 3.46
  certificates, 1.33

National Savings, *cont.*
  13th issue index-linked, 3.39–41
  alternatives to pension schemes, 2.47
  ordinary issue, 3.42
  first option bonds, 3.43
  income bonds, 3.44
  Pensioners' Guaranteed Income Bonds, 3.45
negative equity, mortgage annuity schemes, 6.34
non-residents, holdover relief, 5.17
  income tax treatment, 1.47
notices of coding, adjustments for underpayments, 1.14
  multiple sources of income, 1.7
  widows, 7.35

occupational pension schemes, 2.7–16
  additional voluntary contributions, 2.14
  free-standing, 2.14
  conditions, 2.7
  contributions, employees, 2.12
    maximum, 2.11
  death in service benefits, 2.7, 5.19, 5.39
  defined benefits schemes, 2.9, 3.18
  earnings cap, 2.8
  inflation, provisions, 2.10
  money purchase schemes, 2.9
  options on leaving employment, 2.16
occupational pensions, annuity or lump sum, 2.53
  drawing, timing, 2.53
  income, estimation, 3.4
  PAYE, 1.5
Open-Ended Investment Companies (OEICs), 3.73
overlap relief, 4.13, 4.15
overseas, pensioners living abroad, tax consequences, 1.46–49

parents, gifts in anticipation of marriage, 5.29

partnerships, personal pension schemes, calculation of earnings, 2.22
retirement of partners, income tax, 4.15
succession, 4.41
PAYE, 1.2
notices of coding (*see* **notices of coding**)
pension annuities, 1.5
pension schemes, alternatives, 2.46–50
comparisons, 2.50
death benefits, 5.19
disadvantages, 2.5, 2.41–42
funds, tax credits on dividends, 2.59
taxation, 2.4
importance of early planning, 4.3
occupational pensions, 2.7–16
options, 2.2–6
personal pensions, 2.17–24
retirement annuity pensions, 2.25–29
tax relief, 2.3, 2.46
topping up by companies, before disposal of businesses, 4.38
unapproved retirement benefit schemes, 2.51–52
pensions, drawing, timing, 2.53–68
income, estimation, 3.4–6
tax treatment, 1.4–21
occupational pensions (*see* **occupational pensions**)
personal pensions (*see* **personal pensions**)
state pensions (*see* **state pensions**)
PEPs, 1.33, 3.7, 3.60–65
alternatives to pensions, 2.47
conditions, 3.61
forms, 3.63
limits, 3.60
single-company PEPs, 3.62
personal equity plans, *see* **PEPs**
personal pension schemes, 2.17–24
annuities (*see* **annuities**)

personal pension schemes, *cont.*
benefits, 2.18
death benefits, 2.18, 2.21, 5.19, 5.40
contributions, maximums, 2.20
tax relief, 2.24
disadvantages, 2.41–42
earnings, calculation, 2.22
cap, 2.23, 2.35
entitlement, 2.17
funds, performance, 2.64
group pensions, 2.18
investment links, 2.43–45
joint life pensions, 2.67
retirement annuities, differences, 2.29
interaction, 2.35–40
tax limits, 2.19
unused relief, 2.30–34, 2.38, 2.39, 2.40
personal pensions, income, estimation, 3.5–6
income drawdown, 2.60–65
PAYE, 1.5
phased retirement, 2.56–59, 2.65
PETs, 5.4, 5.5
and holdover relief, 5.16
business property relief, 5.49
CGT liability, 5.8, 5.10
effect on income, 5.9
insurance, 5.43
or deeds of variation, 7.21
reservation of benefits, 5.8, 5.19–21
homes, 5.20
PIBS, 3.54
plant and machinery, business property relief, 5.45
capital allowances, 4.14
potentially exempt transfers, *see* **PETs**
powers of attorney, 7.3, 7.4–6
prior rights, 7.11
purchase of own shares, 4.36

qualifying corporate bonds, 3.55–56

residence, *see also* **non-residents**
executors, 7.32

Index

residence, *cont.*
  meaning, income tax context, 1.48–49
residential care, effect on social security benefits, 6.17
  financing, 6.19–39
    estimate of costs, 6.25
retirement, affordability, 3.3
  age, 3.1
  income (*see* **retirement income**)
  partial retirement, 3.3
retirement annuity pensions, 2.25–29
  benefits, 2.28
    death benefits, 2.27, 5.40
  contributions, maximums, 2.26
  drawing, timing, 2.54
  earnings, calculation, 2.27
    cap, 2.27, 2.35
  income, estimation, 3.5
  investment links, 2.43–45
  PAYE, 1.5
  personal pensions, differences, 2.29
    interaction, 2.35–40
  phased retirement, 2.56–59
  unused relief, 2.30–34, 2.37, 2.39, 2.40
retirement income, 3.3
  estimations, 3.4–10
  topping-up pension income, 3.20–73
retirement relief, 4.19–34
  age, 4.19
  conditions, 4.20–26
  disposal of business or assets, 4.23
  ill health, 4.30
  trust holdings, 4.27–29
  withdrawal, 4.32–34
risk, investments, 3.21, 3.23
rollover relief, 4.35

savings, retirement income, 3.7
self-assessment, 1.10–21
  calculation of tax due, 1.15
    by Inland Revenue, 1.14
  current year, 1.16
  incorrect statements, 1.20

self-assessment, *cont.*
  interest, 1.15
  notification requirements, 1.10–11
    deadline, 1.11
    penalties, 1.11
  payment of tax, 1.15
    late payment, 1.15
  payments on account, 1.17–19
    applications for reduction, 1.19–20
    change of circumstances, 1.19
  surcharges, 1.15
senility, 7.3
SERPS, 2.69, 6.5
shared appreciation mortgages, 6.31
shares, bed and breakfasting, 3.77
  business property relief, 5.45
  disposal, dividends, 4.37
  holdover relief, 5.13
  ISAs, 3.36
  preference shares, 4.42
  purchase of own shares, 4.36
  retirement relief, disposal, 4.22, 4.25
  transfer between spouses, 4.34
  risk, 3.59
  unquoted companies, estimation of income from, 3.9
SHIP, 6.32
social fund, funeral costs, 7.30
social security benefits, after retirement, 6.11–39
  information, 6.18
  reduction, residential and hospital care, 6.17
  safety net, 6.39
sole traders, retirement, 4.16
special destinations, 5.33, 7.8
spouses, capital gains tax, transfer of assets, 3.81, 5.32
  estate tax, 7.25
  income tax, age allowance, 1.30
    personal allowances, 1.24–26
    transfer of allowances, 1.39
  inheritance tax, exemption, 5.30–36
  legal rights, 7.12–18

spouses, *cont.*
  pension annuities, 3.17
  prior rights, 7.11
  retirement relief, transfer of shares, 4.34
  transfer of investment income, 1.35
  will planning, 5.37
stakeholder pensions, 6.2
state pensions, 2.1, 2.69, 6.1–10
  age, 6.3
  deferral, 6.7
  funding, 6.2
  graduated pensions, 6.6
  life expectancy, 6.1
  married women, 6.8
  national insurance contributions, 6.4
  SERPS, 2.69, 6.5
  stakeholder pensions, 6.2
  widows, 6.9
succession, 7.11–18
  businesses, 4.40–42
  legal rights (*see* **legal rights**)
  prior rights, 7.11

taper relief, capital gains tax, 3.78, 4.32
  inheritance tax, 5.5
taxation, *see also* specific taxes
  choice of investments, 3.21, 3.74–75
  disposal of businesses, 4.7
TESSAs, 1.33, 3.7, 3.28–34
  advantages, 3.28
  alternative to pension schemes, 2.47
  assignability, 3.30
  feeder accounts, 3.30
  in ISAs, 3.36, 3.37
  limits, 3.29
  maturity, 3.31
  transfer of accounts, 3.34
  use as securities, 3.30

TESSAs, *cont.*
  withdrawals, interest, 3.34
    within five-year period, 3.32
trustees, charitable trusts, 5.70
  holdover relief, 5.15
trusts, *see also* **accumulation and maintenance trusts; discretionary trusts**
  business assets, business property relief, 5.45
    retirement relief, 4.22, 4.27–29
  capital gains tax, 5.59
  charitable trusts (*see* **charities**)
  gifts of homes to family, 6.22
  holdover relief, 5.18
  liferent trusts, 5.3, 7.25
  use for gifts to children, 5.76

unapproved retirement benefit schemes, 2.51–52
unit trusts, features, 3.67–69
unit-linked policies, pensions, 2.43–45
  estimation of income, 3.6
UURBs, 2.51–52

venture capital trust relief, 4.35

widows, income tax, 7.35
  state pensions, 6.9
  widow's bereavement allowance, 1.40, 7.35
  widow's pension, 6.9, 7.35
wills, 7.7–10
  and legal rights, 7.10, 7.16
  codicils, 7.9
  deeds of variation, 7.10, 7.19–21
  desirability, 7.17
  planning, 5.37–38
  pro forma, 7.9
  professional help, 7.9
winding up, own businesses, 4.4
with-profit policies, pension schemes, 2.43, 2.45